POLITICS OF THE HEART

NONVIOLENCE IN AN AGE OF ATROCITY

Psychedelic
Activism
to End War

ALAN CLEMENTS

WORLD DHARMA PUBLICATIONS

Published in 2026 by
World Dharma Publications
www.WorldDharma.com

Library of Congress Cataloging-in-Publication Data
Clements, Alan, 1951–
*Politics of the Heart: Nonviolence in an Age of Atrocity – Psychedelic Activism and
the End of War* by Alan Clements.
p. cm.

ISBN 978-1-953508-36-2

Myanmar—Politics and government—2021–present
Military dictatorship—Psychological aspects
Human rights—Myanmar
Resistance movements—Myanmar
Freedom—Political and philosophical perspectives
Authoritarianism—Global impact
Aung San Suu Kyi—Political imprisonment
Revolution—Nonviolent and armed resistance
Consciousness—Political and ethical dimensions
Global justice—Political and environmental activism
Social movements—Democracy and human rights

First printing, January 1, 2026
ISBN 978-1-953508-36-2

PREFACE

The Why of This Book

We are living in an age of engineered atrocity—an empire of *normalized* ruin and moral anesthesia. The unthinkable has become *ordinary*; the intolerable now speaks in policy. Children are incinerated beneath drones while leaders dine in distant mansions—possessed by the cold euphoria of impunity. The camera rolls, the markets rise, and the algorithms hum—translating carnage into content, blood into data, tragedy into metrics, and conscience into commodities.

This is *the banality of evil* reborn—not in camps but in clouds. What Hannah Arendt once saw in the bureaucrat's tidy desk has metastasized into a planetary operating system: war streamlined by bandwidth, propaganda rebranded as news, and morality outsourced to branding. We are witnessing the torture of language—words bent to justify the unthinkable, truth asphyxiated into "balance," and freedom repurposed as "security."

And yet, beneath this global hypnosis, a deeper war rages—the war for consciousness itself. The ancient struggle between awareness and ignorance, between empathy and erasure, has migrated to the digital frontier. We are no longer merely ruled; we are programmed. Authoritarianism no longer knocks at the door; it auto-plays. The algorithm has become the new altar, demanding its sacrifices in data.

Illusion, the state's favorite narcotic, now floods the feed. No books need be burned; only discernment. Attention suffocates, and awareness becomes contraband.

This book was written as an act of conscience—not as commentary, not as confession, nor philosophy, but as witness. It arose from the slow accumulation of *moral shock*—from seeing too much, feeling too much, and realizing that silence had become a form of consent. I did not choose to write it. The words arrived like survivors—wounded, insistent, demanding asylum.

I have spent decades documenting the cruelty of systems, studying dictatorships, and listening to the fear in ordinary hearts. I have watched how freedom is murdered not by tyrants alone but by exhaustion, cynicism, and the temptation to look away. In the end, I understood that the front line is not geographic but interior. The true battleground is perception—the contested ground between attention and amnesia.

Awareness has become rebellion. To remain lucid amid concocted confusion is now a political statement. To feel deeply is a form of resistance. To tell the truth—without permission—is a revolution of the spirit. This book, then, is not revelation but reclamation—the repossession of our own seeing, the recognition that a mind, once cleared and empowered by mindful discernment, is no longer deceivable.

And if I may add, with humble directness, clarity has never been so out of style—or so subversive. As Wilde might have said, nothing ruins a perfectly good illusion quite like *the naked arrival of truth*.

The Lineage of Works

This work stands beside two companions—*Conversation with a Dictator: A Challenge to the Authoritarian Assault* and *Unsilenced: Aung San Suu Kyi—Conversations from a Myanmar Prison*. Together, they form a moral trilogy—a cartography of conscience that maps tyranny, endurance, and awakening across the psychic landscape of our species.

Conversation with a Dictator is an Orwellian descent—a forensic plunge into the unraveling psyche of power on the brink of collapse. It unfolds as an imagined dialogue with Burma's coup leader, General Min Aung Hlaing—a man armored in delusion, commanding obedience yet imprisoned by fear. The book forces him toward the mirror he avoids—

toward the moment when language revolts against its liar. It reads like the final hour before rebirth in hell—the narrow interval when the mask cracks and the buried conscience claws back into awareness. Through this lens, power reveals itself not as strength but as spectacle—a fevered theater concealing the terror of self-recognition.

In this sense, *Conversation with a Dictator* is less a political tract than psychological exorcism—a mirror held up to the architecture of domination, compelling the tyrant to witness the slow corrosion of his own humanity.

Unsilenced is its mirror and its mercy—a meditative, imagined series of in-depth conversations with Aung San Suu Kyi, Myanmar's Nobel Peace Laureate, speaking from solitary confinement, her voice stripped of all but dignity and conscience. Where the dictator rationalizes violence and power, she responds with presence—mindful silence distilled into spiritual lucidity. In the stillness of captivity, she radiates the ferocity of compassion—a *Dharma power* no prison can extinguish, no darkness contain, no propaganda defile.

If the dictator's voice is a requiem for empathy, hers is its resurrection—an illumination of what remains unbroken within the human spirit, even under total constraint.

Politics of the Heart completes the arc—the passage from delusion to awakening, from domination to discernment. If *Conversation with a Dictator* exposes how power collapses under the weight of its own deceit, and *Unsilenced* embodies the stillness that survives it, then this book is the act of rebellion that follows awareness—the refusal to descend, the decision to create. It is the convergence of philosophy, activism, and art—a field manual for the *revolution of the spirit*. Here, freedom is not ideology but intimacy; not the possession of a nation, but *the awakening of perception itself—the restoration of moral imagination to public life, and the return of empathy to power.*

The Origin of My Conviction

My life has unfolded on the fault line between monasteries and frontlines—between the precision of meditation and the chaos of political upheaval. As a Buddhist monk under Mahasi Sayadaw and Sayadaw U Pandita, I was trained to observe the mind without flinching—to see how craving and fear masquerade as reason, how delusion manufactures its own necessity. Later, as a journalist expelled from Burma for documenting its atrocities, I witnessed those same forces externalized—organized into armies, legislated into cruelty, normalized through fear.

Through decades alongside prisoners of conscience and survivors of dictatorship, I came to understand a truth no ideology could contain: authoritarianism is not merely a system—it is a reflex of consciousness. It begins within as perception and thrives wherever empathy dies. Once absorbed into the psyche, it requires no tyrant to sustain it. We internalize the oppressor—becoming *the archivists of our own submission*, the curators of our own diminishment.

The antidote cannot be purely political; it must be existential—psychological, moral, and spiritual. It must address the architecture of delusion before it ossifies into law. The revolution begins not in protest but in perception—in the ungoverned interior where attention and ethics converge. For it is there that meditation becomes governance—the quiet rule of the inner republic—and loving-kindness rises as the most radical act of civil disobedience.

The Pulse Beneath the Words

Politics of the Heart is not a manual of solutions but a meditation on sacred responsibility—an invocation to protect the interior world from being colonized by fear and noise. Its purpose is not to persuade but to awaken—to remind us that clarity is not luxury; it is our oxygen.

The subtitle, *Nonviolence in an Age of Atrocity,* defines the ethical spine of the work. Nonviolence is not restraint but lucid and *creative defiance—the disciplined refusal to internalize domination*. It transforms conscience into a form of power unreachable by cruelty.

And the companion phrase, *Psychedelic Activism and the End of War,* gestures toward something older and more radical than politics: a re-enchantment of perception itself. Here, the psychedelic is not chemical but spiritual—the restoration of wonder to its rightful place as moral intelligence. To see reality unfiltered is to remember that empathy and intelligence are not rivals but refractions of the same lucid awareness. Awakening is not escape; it is participation raised to the sacred—an exquisite involvement in the living world.

If tyranny begins as a contraction of consciousness, then awakening—perceptual, ethical, spiritual—becomes its unraveling, its widening back into truth and tenderness. This book is therefore both field report and vow: a testament to where humanity fractures, and to what still rises whenever conscience refuses captivity.

Reader's Compact

This book asks three things: *attention, imagination,* and *mercy. Attention*— to notice when your mind is being outsourced or anesthetized without consent. *Imagination*—to picture a world where harm is not inevitable but unlearned and undone. *Mercy*—to begin again when you fail, and to let others begin again when they do. Hold these three close, and the reading becomes a meditation on freedom—a dialogue between awareness and the world that would forget it.

To the Reader

This work is not written from a place of distance but from spiritual debt—to those who risked everything for truth, who suffered without surrendering their humanity. Their endurance taught me what no scripture could: *compassion is the final form of intelligence, and awareness remains the last sanctuary of freedom.*

I offer this book to them, and to you—to all who keep their hearts open in an age that tempts us to turn away. May it serve as a reminder that sanity is not consensus but courage; that love is not sentiment, but discipline; and that awakening is not withdrawal, but full engagement with reality—*unarmed, undefended, and awake.*

In the end, no ideology contains the wild fact of being human. There is only awareness—alive, vivid, unbranded, and free.

Thank you for walking this path with me.
—Alan Clements, 2026

INTRODUCTION

The Theatre of Freedom in an Age of Consciousness Warfare

"Hatred never ceases by hatred, but only by love; this is the eternal law."
— The *Dhammapada,* (attributed to the Buddha)

❈

*N*irvāṇa is not a destination—it is the river of awareness, deliberately eroding violence.

This book began as an act of conscience—a current of creative awareness veiled as an evening of politicized art. It was late summer 2025, in a small studio in *Haʻikū*, Maui—the air charged with that quiet electricity which signals something larger than performance was about to stir. It was not art as escape, but language reborn as risk—as unveiled conscience, as truth struggling to speak in an age deafened by its own echo.

The event was titled *Dictatorship, Democracy, Dharma, and the Insanity of War,* the launch of my new illustrated novel, *Conversation with a Dictator: A Challenge to the Authoritarian Assault.* But what unfolded that night defied self-censorship. It could not be contained by a title or single book. It expanded into an invocation—*Politics of the Heart: Nonviolence in an Age of Atrocity—Psychedelic Activism and the End of War.*

They came not for spectacle but for presence—artists, thinkers, seekers, and friends who had endured the long exhaustion of recent years and still carried, however quietly, a belief in the sanctity of awareness. They gathered as witnesses—to conscience, to language, to that fragile miracle: a frail attempt at truth spoken aloud in an age of hyper-polarization.

The Core Theme

If we do not end violence, violence will end us. But the question—the burning question—is this: *what within us will awaken before it's too late?*

That night, words came naked—stripped of cliché and ceremony. Thought courted feeling; irony held hands with grief. The air trembled—not with faith, but with the quiet recognition of raw, tender truths reclaiming their right to shape the space we share—the fragile republic of freedom and democracy: *the politics of the heart.*

I had not come to entertain, but to invite participation in something older than politics—the living root from which all true politics must arise: *the freedom to think, to feel, to speak without permission.* Perhaps it was theatre, yes, but theatre in its original sense—a civic ritual of remembrance, where ideas and emotions meet in the open air of democracy. As Wilde once said, *"Sincerity is far too rare a thing to be taken literally,"* yet that night, sincerity itself felt revolutionary—a quiet defiance against the algorithm of indifference.

That evening was not rebellion but renewal—for me, at least—a long-awaited reawakening of moral and *dharmically inspired imagination*. It reminded me, and perhaps all of us, that freedom of expression, when offered in good faith, is not performance but communion—a way of loving the world through honesty.

This is the essence of the politics of the heart: where awareness becomes activism, love becomes intelligence, and truth—stripped of ornament and ideology—learns again to breathe.

The New Architecture of Power

We are living through a war most cannot see—fought not on battlefields but in browsers, not for territory but for attention. We now stand at the crossroads of biology and bandwidth—between the ancestral and the algorithmic, between consciousness and code. The weapons are invisible—data, images, narratives. The terrain is the human nervous system. This is *consciousness warfare*—the silent occupation of awareness by psychological and technological means.

In the twentieth century, tyrants built prisons of concrete; in the twenty-first, they build prisons of perception. They no longer burn books; they flood the mind with glittering trivia. *Authoritarianism has gone wireless*. It no longer needs the whip or the wall—only *the feed*. The algorithm is the new dictator—invisible, tireless, and disturbingly intimate.

The strategy is simple: overwhelm, fragment, exhaust. Keep citizens reactive but never reflective. Train us to mistake reaction for thought, performance for participation, hysteria for agency. In such a climate, cruelty is rebranded as compassion, domination is marketed as democracy. Moral inversion is the signature technology of modern power—*laundering harm through the language of virtue*.

What Buddhism calls *papanca*—the proliferation of thought and craving—has become industrialized. Capital now monetizes the three poisons: greed, hatred, and delusion. Each click strengthens the machine. Each moment of distraction surrenders a measure of sovereignty.

And yet a subversive truth persists: *the colonized mind can still be decolonized*. Awareness—ungoverned clarity—is the antidote. The instant we recognize manipulation, the spell begins to dissolve. In that moment, consciousness ceases to be an object of exploitation and remembers its origin—the one domain tyrants can never occupy.

This book, then, is not a lament but a manual for *perceptual freedom—the right to one's own mind*. It is, in spirit, *a guide to the politics of the heart*, where seeing clearly itself becomes an act of nonviolence.

Consciousness Warfare: The Battle for the Human Mind

Consciousness warfare is the state religion of the algorithmic age—a borderless empire shaping what we think, feel, and dream. It is not fought with bullets but with symbols, not with armies but with algorithms. The field of battle is the psyche, and the prize, human imagination. Consciousness has become the final frontier of policy.

In Freudian terms, we are witnessing the mass production of repression—desire and dread outsourced to systems that feed them back as spectacle. The id is interactive. The superego, automated. The ego scrolls in endless loops of comparison and despair. The marketplace has replaced the analyst; confession has become content.

Jung might have said we are drowning in our collective shadow—the unintegrated drives of greed, dominance, and fear projected onto others, replayed in every polarized narrative. The unconscious, once explored through dreams, now lives inside the algorithm—training itself on our impulses, building mirror-worlds where we perform instead of awaken.

The Buddha would recognize the same war: craving (*tanhā*) versus awareness (*sati*). What was once called *Māra*—the tempter who diverts the mind from seeing clearly—now glows from our screens. The entire apparatus of distraction is the modern face of delusion.

What Freud called repression, Jung the shadow, and the Buddha ignorance, now converge in one machinery: technology externalizing the unconscious and curating blindness for profit. What was once an inner battlefield has become the architecture of empire.

To understand consciousness warfare is to understand that *totalitarianism begins in perception*. When reflection erodes, compassion becomes optional. When attention is harvested, ethics become negotiable. When imagination is captured, tyranny no longer needs coercion—only consent disguised as convenience.

And yet awareness remains the one power they cannot own. Every mindful moment is rebellion. Every refusal to react on command reclaims sovereignty. The coming revolution will not be fought for ideology but for inner freedom—the right to think and feel without manipulation.

In this war, art, love, and *Dhamma* are instruments of resistance. They re-enchant perception—making life vivid again. For the most radical act is still this: to stay awake—*to inhabit one's own consciousness as liberated territory.*

The Keepers of the Trance

If consciousness warfare is the empire's strategy, capitalism is its temple—and its high priests are the keepers of the trance. They do not rule by force but by fascination. Their dominion is not land but perception. Their power depends on keeping the world half-awake—entranced by illusion, numbed by choice, sedated by convenience.

We call it "the economy," but it is more precisely a *psychic marketplace*—a theater of craving where value is measured not in worth but attention itself. Every click, every purchase, every distraction becomes an offering laid to the invisible gods of desire. They are *the merchants of forgetting*—selling us shards of our own stolen time.

The spell is subtle: a trance of normalcy— the illusion that this system's poisoned rivers, burning forests, and exhausted souls are inevitable. Yet even within the fog, something ancient stirs. The trance flickers. The dreamers begin to wake up.

As Charles Finch writes, *"In some sense, capitalism is already behind us... All of it serves the pathological greed of a few thousand mentally ill men. It cannot last."*

The keepers of the trance know this. They feel the scaffolding tremble. They sense that the mythology of endless growth is dying—not from revolution, but from exhaustion. So, they amplify distraction, accelerate the feed, and weaponize despair—hoping sedation will outlast conscience.

But awakening is contagious. Lucidity spreads like wildfire through dry fields of apathy. To see the trance is to weaken it. What breaks the spell is not outrage but clarity—the recognition that *sanity is a revolution.*

To live *trans-politically* is to refuse the trance in every costume—capitalist, nationalist, spiritual, ideological. It is to move through illusion toward integrity, through spectacle toward sincerity. *The trans-political mind knows that every domination system endures only by our consent to believe in it.*

The coming revolution will not be a war of classes but a recovery of consciousness. It will not overthrow capitalism by force but dissolve its psychic infrastructure—the trance of scarcity, the addiction to dominance, the worship of accumulation. It will replace consumption with communion, extraction with reverence, obedience with awareness.

This is not utopia but evolutionary necessity. The keepers will lose not by defeat but by remembrance—that *the world was never theirs to own.*

The real wealth is aliveness. The real currency is attention. *The most radical defiance is to awaken—fully, mercifully, together.*

The politics of the heart begins here—in the refusal to be hypnotized by power and in the remembrance that empathy, too, is intelligence.

Nonviolence in the Age of Atrocity

I have seen what happens when conscience collapses. I have walked through burned villages in Burma, stood beside mothers digging graves with their hands, and listened to the prayers of monks whose monasteries had become morgues. I have seen what imagination becomes when infected by hatred.

But I have also seen the opposite: the quiet ferocity of those who refuse to hate. I have sat with men and women who had been tortured for years, yet walked out of prison with their humanity intact. They did not win in any conventional sense, yet they carried a victory no regime could annul—the refusal to become what they opposed.

That is the meaning of nonviolence—not passivity or moral luxury, but the disciplined refusal to internalize the logic of harm. It is the art of remaining tender in a world gone numb—the courage to breathe with the world instead of against it. *It begins in listening*—the kind that stills the inner noise until one can hear the heartbeat of another, the wing-beat of a bird, the hush of a tree bending to the wind. *Nonviolence is how the earth itself teaches: through patience, renewal, and the unspoken vow to keep giving life.*

Nonviolence is not only the refusal to strike, but the refusal to profit from harm. It calls out the slow violence of neglect—the sanctioned cruelties of hunger, poverty, and exclusion that masquerade as policy. To practice nonviolence today is to see clearly the machinery of suffering—economic, digital, psychological—and to withdraw one's consent.

It is to speak softly to the unseen—to the cloud passing, the stray dog at the door, the soil beneath the feet—and to know that everything listens back. It is the conversation beneath all conversations, where words yield to awareness and respect becomes the grammar of being.

To live this way is to practice *sacred restraint*—the pause before intrusion, the breath before speech, the reverence that asks permission of all things. *Nonviolence is how love moves when it no longer needs to prove itself.* It is how consciousness bows before existence, recognizing that nothing is separate—that to harm another is to harm one's own self.

It is not a philosophy of opposition but of participation—the willingness to be woven into the living fabric of the world with care. To tend what grows. To mend what breaks. To offer presence where pain has made others vanish.

At its essence, nonviolence means this: to be kind when no one is watching, to listen as if the universe were speaking through each fragile moment, to meet what is before you with the quiet power of love that neither clings nor turns away.

This is not weakness; it is the strength that does not shout—the silence that restores, the still beauty that gathers all things into wholeness again.

Nonviolence is mindfulness flowering into love—the restoration of the sacred within the ordinary. It is how the world begins to heal through us, one gentle act at a time, until even the air remembers it is holy.

Psychedelic Activism and the Re-Enchantment of Consciousness

The word *psychedelic* means "mind-manifesting." It refers not only to substances but to a way of perceiving: direct, unfiltered, alive. *Psychedelic activism*, as I use it here, is not about drugs but about perception—awakening from the consensual trance of obedience.

The dominant hallucination of our age is *normalcy*—the narcotic illusion that violence, inequality, and ecological collapse are inevitable. Psychedelic activism is the refusal of that hallucination—a moral insurgency against the domestication of wonder. It begins in perception and ends in empathy, for *to see deeply is to care deeply.*

True psychedelic awareness is not escapist; it is radically awake to reality. It dissolves numbness and rekindles awe—the one force tyranny cannot domesticate. In every age, oppressors have renamed submission as order, conquest as civilization, numbness as peace. Psychedelic activism is the refusal of that hypnosis. A people who still marvel at life cannot kneel before fear.

This is why the psychedelic, the artistic, and the spiritual converge in acts of conscience. They open the door to what Václav Havel called the *power of the powerless*—truth lived without permission. They remind us that liberation begins not in legislation but in imagination. The end of war, if it comes, will be envisioned by poets and mystics—those who dare to feel everything.

War is the failure of imagination; peace its triumph.

The Emergence of the Trans-Political

And so, we arrive at the impasse of the present: a civilization both hyperconnected and spiritually starved. Public life has become a theatre of binaries—left and right, believer and skeptic, woke and asleep—each side convinced it owns reality. Politics has devolved into a spectacle of managed outrage, a digital coliseum where conviction is performed for the algorithms and outrage is mistaken for participation.

Out of this exhaustion, as mentioned earlier, another possibility emerges—*the trans-political.* The word trans means through, not above. It implies passage, not transcendence. To live trans-politically is to move through ideology toward conscience, through identity toward universality, through language toward silence. It is to cross the boundaries that divide us without erasing the differences that make us human. It is not neutrality but fidelity to truth wherever it appears.

The trans-political citizen refuses both cynicism and fanaticism. They know that democracy without mindfulness becomes propaganda, and freedom without compassion degenerates into narcissism. They see that sovereignty—personal, national, spiritual—begins in *the integrity of attention.* To reclaim one's mind is the first act of self-governance.

They understand that the health of democracy is not measured by unanimity but by the courage to think without applause. They do not withdraw from the world; they re-enter it more awake. They embody what I call the *revolution of the spirit*—activism practiced as meditation, dissent conducted with grace.

This revolution begins within. The trans-political is not a rejection of politics but its renewal—the restoration of conscience to public life, the return of empathy to the vocabulary of power. It asks not, *"Which side are you on?"* but *"What truth are you serving?"*

This orientation demands a new literacy: *the literacy of awareness*—to discern what is real from what is rehearsed, to feel without manipulation, to think without the permission of one's tribe. It is *the discipline of sanity in an age of insanity*—the capacity to hold contradiction without losing compassion.

The trans-political is not theory but a posture of consciousness—an ethics of seeing that restores humanity to the field of politics. It is the marriage of discernment and empathy, intellect and heart, rebellion and reverence. It is the art of staying human within systems that reward forgetfulness—the daily practice of democracy as awareness in action.

Freedom as a Spiritual Discipline

The phrase *Choose Humanity Over Insanity* is not a slogan but a spiritual diagnosis. It names the fracture running through the modern psyche—between conscience and conditioning, perception and propaganda. To choose humanity is to remember aliveness amid automation—to insist that *sanity is sacred, empathy is intelligence,* and *awareness is revolutionary.*

Every page that follows is written as both confession and call to arms—not for battle, but for presence. In an age of mechanized minds, attention itself becomes an act of love. Nonviolence begins in perception; it is the refusal to perceive through fear. From that clarity, responsibility follows—the understanding that peace is not bestowed by institutions but built, breath by breath, through the courage of ordinary people.

This is what I learned in Burma, in exile, and in that small studio in Maui: *freedom is not granted by governments but cultivated in the depths of the heart.* It is the capacity to remain lucid in madness, compassionate in cruelty, and awake in seduction.

If we can preserve that—if we can keep the mind free and the imagination alive—humanity endures, even amid atrocity.

That is the wager. That is the prayer. That is our chance—to begin again, to choose humanity over insanity—*the enduring politics of the heart.*

— Alan Clements, 2026

DEDICATION

To the people of Myanmar—
the dissidents and the dreamers,
the fearless and the fallen,
those who rise with only dignity,
and refuse to bow.

To Daw Aung San Suu Kyi—
whose conscience remains unbroken,
a beacon in darkness.

To the 22,000 dissident prisoners—
enduring the bars of silence,
keeping the pulse of truth alive.

To the mothers, the monks, the students,
the rebels with empty hands
and unbreakable spirits.

To the exiles who carry their homeland in their hearts.

To the children—bright flames of tomorrow, whose laughter prophesies
freedom, whose innocence demands a world beyond war, beyond
hunger, beyond despair.

To the unborn—silent heirs of possibility, entrusted with the dawn of
a civilization not yet imagined, where their first breath is not stolen by
chains but carried on winds of liberty.

To every soul who refuses tyranny—across nations, across generations,
across time—risking everything not merely for the liberation of a
single nation, but for the birth of a future where conscience outshines
cruelty, imagination outruns fear, and dignity is not a dream but the
air we all must breathe.

This book is for you.
This book is because of you.
This book is a vow carved into the marrow of history—offered to the
living, the lost, and the yet to be born.

And one day—beyond barbed wire,
beyond propaganda,
beyond fear—
freedom will rise not as an idea but as a new world.

And when it does, you will not be remembered as victims, but as visionaries, architects of an earth restored, guardians of its children, and midwives of an awakening that will not die.

The Immortality of Kindness

"I have seen that it is not man who is impotent in the struggle against evil, but the power of evil that is impotent in the struggle against man. The powerlessness of kindness, of senseless kindness, is the secret of its immortality. It can never by conquered. The more stupid, the more senseless, the more helpless it may seem, the vaster it is. Evil is impotent before it. The prophets, religious teachers, reformers, social and political leaders are impotent before it. This dumb, blind love is man's meaning. Human history is not the battle of good struggling to overcome evil. It is a battle fought by a great evil, struggling to crush a small kernel of human kindness. But if what is human in human beings has not been destroyed even now, then evil will never conquer."

Vasily Grossman, *Life and Fate*

Table of Contents

Part I:

COLLAPSE

Section I:
The Insurrection of the Spirit

Awonder. A privilege. A *holy gift*—to arrive in this gathering, in this unrepeatable moment with you. Thank you—and thank you, Tom, Michelle—for helping shape this sanctuary of conscience and communion tonight.

To speak here is not performance but a kind of consecration— or, at the very least, my best attempt at one. A vow. A pledge to truth unmasked. Not seduced by self-censorship, I pray. Not captured by commodified outrage, I hope. But a risk—an insurrection of the spirit: *a politics of the heart.*

I did not come to be ordinary. Nor to be tamed by the opioid we call safety. As we know, safety—the psychic sedation of our age, the morphine of conformity—lulls us into obedience: well-mannered, existentially paralyzed. Perfect citizens. Perfectly useless. Like aging housecats at the end of empire. And yes, I love safety; I just refuse to overdose on it. So, we sleepwalk—tranquilized, compliant—while the world burns.

And if it makes you nervous, please relax—at least I didn't bring a PowerPoint deck. I'm a spiritually incorrect, extemporaneous spoken-word ex-Buddhist monk—equal parts spectrum and psychedelic, afflicted with a chronic case of irreverence and excessive-mindfulness disorder—hardly a merchant of mediocrity hustling for clients.

And if I may add, the only thing worse than offending the powerful is boring the powerless. That, my friends, is my offering. If it unsettles, good. If it comforts, forgive me—I'll try harder next time.

The Theatre of Self-Betrayal

Carl Jung once wrote a line that has never left me: *"People suffer most not from the cruelties of the world, but from the betrayal of their own unlived life."*

And I find myself paraphrasing him, because I see it everywhere: it is not the world alone that wounds us, but the life we refuse to live.

Yes, there are those who suffer the unspeakable torments of war, torture, and starvation—the brutalities no psyche should have to bear. Yet even among them, and perhaps especially among them, the inner betrayal still cuts deepest: the dimming of one's own light, the silencing of one's own song.

The unlived life doesn't vanish; it ferments. It turns sour, thickens into bitterness, sharpens into contempt, and hardens into rigidity.

If we are not vigilant, if we are not mindful—then we slip into pretending. We let self-betrayal disguise itself as safety. We mistake mimicry for belonging. We inherit illusions and call them the authentic life. We perform instead of live. We follow scripts instead of improvise. *We mimic freedom while quietly colluding with captivity.*

Freedom is rarely stolen; more often, we return it politely, like a library book we never bothered to read. That, to me, is what Jung was pointing at: the corrosion that comes not only from external tyranny, but from within—when we abandon the dangerous possibility of becoming who we are and settle instead for the parade of pretending.

Erotic *Ubuntu*: The Creative Voltage of Being

He was right. What corrodes us is not only injustice from without, but betrayal from within—the refusal of our own uncharted adventure, obedience to shadows on the walls of our own consciousness, mistaken for daylight.

Here we wake from the trance of self-betrayal—unarmored, naked, embodied in what I call *eroticized ubuntu*: erotic not as sex, but as the pulse and vow of an unprogrammed life—the fierce intimacy of being unrepeatably alive together, tangled and tender in the experiment of freedom.

Most people don't fear death; they fear naked naturalness—erotic authenticity, spontaneity, improvisation—life refusing the unfelt trauma of a fossilized script. Refuse it and you mimic parody; embrace it and you risk everything—the vulnerability of sacred presence, the danger of truth, the tenderness of beauty. Anything less is embalming—a monument to one's own betrayal.

The Commerce of Contempt: Mockery as the Mask of the Unlived Life

Let me press the point further: the artist who never makes art becomes cynical about those who do. The lover who never risks loving mocks romance. The thinker who never commits to a philosophy sneers at belief itself. And yet all of them suffer, because deep down they know: the life they mock is the life they were meant to live.

That word—*mock*—matters. Because mockery—ridicule, scorn, derision, contempt—has become the *lingua franca* of culture. Leaders who cannot dream mock the dreamers. Politicians who cannot love mock compassion. Commentators who cannot create mock creation itself.

Entire industries now profit from sneer and derision, weaponizing bitterness into spectacle—and, in the darkest theatre, leaders stoop to mock genocide, dismissing it as mere collateral damage in the crusade to eradicate evil.

I know mockery well—it's what I reached for when courage felt too costly. Behind every act of mockery lies the same wound: the unlived life, the abandoned possibility. And deeper still, self-loathing—and its most glorified disguise: narcissism. And perhaps its most celebrated form, sociopathy—the insecurity of the infant fused with the political savagery of a viper. Dictatorship—just the toddler tantrum with better PR.

Manufactured Identity, Monetized Outrage

Today, a single word can fracture a family. One sentence can ignite a nation. Speak one way, and you're erased; speak another and you're exalted. The whiplash is instantaneous: love me, cancel me, worship me, destroy me. Don't answer a text on time and it's betrayal. Don't consent to another's ignorance of boundaries, and it's war—ghosting, exile, digital assassination.

We've mistaken reaction for relationship, performance for presence, visibility for connection. The new heresy is nuance; the new sin, hesitation. And in this age of perpetual display, silence itself has become an act of rebellion.

This isn't merely the absurdity of our age—it's its pathology: truth skinned alive and resold as ideology. I'm right, you're wrong. You're insane, I'm sane. What begins as disagreement mutates into identity war, each side nourished by the other's vilification—or its justified estrangement.

Welcome to the algorithmic funhouse mirror: individuality pre-fabricated, emotion commodified, thinking outsourced. The politics of division aren't a glitch—they're the system's design. To keep us fractured is to keep us controllable; to keep us yelling is to keep us blind.

Oh my. Forgive the aside—either it's my Tourette's kicking in, or withdrawal from performative-authenticity fatigue.

Samsara in the Age of Algorithms

Or, as my *Dharma* teachers in Burma reminded us: *Welcome to Samsara*— the cycle of self-inflicted suffering, now upgraded with push notifications as we microdose. A realm where craving is repackaged as "mindful choice," hatred rebranded as "healing strength," and delusion streamed live—until the gods of our own making rise to feast upon us and the earth itself becomes their altar.

In the old texts, *samsara was a wheel of rebirth*; today, it is a feed you cannot stop scrolling—endlessly refreshing, endlessly consuming. It isn't the generals alone, nor the corporations, nor the politicians who imprison us; *we collaborate in our own captivity*—one click, one outrage, one reflex of algorithmic self-betrayal at a time.

The difference between a monastery and a feed? In one, you watch your mind. In the other, your mind is watched—and harvested.

The Third World War isn't theoretical; it's internal. We are already in it—living inside its code. It unfolds not on battlefields but in attention spans, in nervous systems, in the soft tissue of thought itself.

Welcome to *consciousness warfare.*

Welcome to *digital samsara.*

From Self-Betrayal to the Raw Dignity of Freedom

Here Jung's warning returns: the unlived life congeals into bitterness, rigidity, and contempt. The artist who never creates, the lover who never risks, the leader who never leads—all mock what they secretly ache for: originality, freedom, intimacy, ungoverned passion.

And beneath it all lies the most exiled hunger of all—the soul's longing for the sacred: that faint stirring when beauty startles the ordinary, when presence deepens and the familiar grows transparent. To deny that is to fossilize in slow motion. To surrender to it is to be quietly carried toward *the radiance of awe*—that fragile interval when the self loosens its grip and being itself begins to breathe through us.

And in our time, that hunger is not merely forgotten—it is *harvested.* The machinery of modern life feeds on our exile from wonder, offering simulations of meaning where reverence once lived. Attention—presence infused with curiosity and heart—has become the rarest form of intimacy.

The Humility of Nuance

And let me admit this: phrases like *"fully alive"* or *"radiance of awe"* can too easily become clichés—easy to preach, easy to market, easier still to hide behind. Their true meaning—their direct experience, like a flowing, rippling river—is far more elusive, more demanding: an infinite spectrum of nuance.

It reveals itself in the quiet choreography of being. Sometimes it looks like art. Sometimes it looks like awe. Sometimes it looks like telling the truth when it costs you. Sometimes it looks like silence when silence protects. Sometimes it looks like laughter in the ruins, or tenderness in a moment of despair.

To be fully alive is not to chase an idealized behavior, but to inhabit the ten thousand gestures of a life that is opening, unbetrayed. That's *the humility of nuance.* That's the radiance of freedom—not an ideal to perform, but a living possibility: fragile, perilous, sacred—always ours to risk.

For me, *freedom is gradation itself*—the aesthetics of living with discernment and choice—or it is nothing. And freedom, like the wind: the moment you try to define, capture, or claim it, it slips through the net of language.

Freedom Against the Machine

I'll continue with our beloved Oscar Wilde, who once said: *"Disobedience, in the eyes of anyone who has read history, is man's original virtue."* And I think he was right. *Disobedience—moral courage in motion, the refusal to conform to the lie.*

Not mere defiance, but the quiet intelligence that keeps truth alive between conformity and collapse. It isn't about being for or against, obedient or rebellious, but about how we move—the mindful tension between contraction and expansion, between performance and authenticity. Without that tension, there is no change, no freedom, no art, no truth. And without it, you don't even get rock 'n' roll—

just patriarchy, domination, or neurotic self-regulation: a disguised conformity, your own self-censoring digital ID.

And so, I gather with you tonight not to rehearse, not to flatter, but to be raw. Unscripted. Disruptive. To risk a little conscious disorder in pursuit of something resembling truth. Not a tidy TED Talk from *Truth, Inc.*, complete with a slide deck and a standing ovation for simulated authenticity—but the unruly kind. The barefoot, unfiltered, truth-that-bites-you-in-the-ass truth—the one that stains your reputation, rearranges your friendships, and ruins your brand deals before setting you free.

And please, do not mistake my restless cadence for evasion. I am a man who never mastered boundaries, who spent years in monasteries dissolving them—only to return to a Western world obsessed with fortifying them: walls, borders, gated hearts. Awakening, which once felt elemental, suddenly seemed untranslatable—packaged down into wellness porn, mindfulness-on-demand, enlightenment™ for hire, *tantra* on subscription—half-off in January.

And now, my own signature line of trauma-informed yoga mats, each with an AI-administered squirt of ketamine nasal spray to wake you up for your extended corpse pose.

Offended? Good. I warned you. Boundaries and I are still on non-speaking terms. And maybe that's why I can say this without flinching: the moment freedom becomes a business model—it isn't freedom at all—it's captivity with better marketing. And the brochure always looks better than the prison cell.

Trans-Political: Outside the Map

Am I saying I'm not political? No—quite the opposite. I see nothing separate from politics. Freedom is not an island; it is the air we breathe, together. But I am not defined by the categories on offer. Not left, not right, not even center. Those coordinates are broken, relics, no longer describing reality.

I stand outside the map—*trans-political*, or, as I said earlier, *a politics of the heart*. Beyond the counterfeit binary. Beyond the algorithmic echo chambers that impersonate thought, recycling division into identity, mistaking noise for principle. Beyond the engineered tribalism that conditions us to confuse sides with truth—or worse, to doom-scroll our souls into prescription refills.

When every feed is programmed to provoke, sovereignty of mind becomes the new punk. To refuse digital hypnosis is not retreat—it's rebellion. It's deleting the algorithm before it deletes your intuition; choosing presence over performance, signal over noise. To think for yourself—outside the Biometric Data Collection Project of the corporate-political mindlords—is now the rarest freedom.

And here in America, where the First Amendment was meant to safeguard choice, sovereignty, and conscience, that refusal is not naïve idealism. It's survival—a sacred glitch in the matrix, a jailbreak of attention, a quiet uprising of the awake.

Do not mistake my stance for neutrality, or for some culturally chic way of performing transcendent divinity. I am not outside politics; I am within it—aware, awake, incarnate—yet beyond the box it's been sold in, rooted instead in the living fusion of the *Dharma*—the law of conscience, of interdependence, of awakening—with the articles of freedom enshrined in the Universal Declaration of Human Rights.

But let me say this more plainly: those rights are not mere legalities. They are *the Dharma of dignity*—the breath of love, the heart-compass of our becoming. They are the soil beneath our feet—fertile, fragile, alive with possibility. They are not an ornament of civilization but its pulse— the journey of liberation itself.

A Dharma-Inspired Declaration of Interbeing

And if you're wondering where I stand—what I believe—let me lay it bare. Not a party platform. Not a brand. But *a dharma-inspired declaration of interbeing*. A living manifesto for the heart. Ten freedoms I carry as marrow and breath—freedoms anyone, anywhere, can claim. Freedoms born of *mindful intelligence*, of *sacred reciprocity*, of *eroticized ubuntu*—the felt truth that my aliveness, my very existence, is intimately, inseparably bound with yours. *A politics of the heart.*

The first is the *freedom of thought*—to think clearly, without coercion, censorship, or the chokehold of conformity. *To know your own mind*, because to know your mind is the most important task of a human life. Without it, all other freedoms collapse.

The second is the *freedom of conscience*—to dissent, to refuse complicity in cruelty, to say no when no one else will. To honor that still small voice within, the inner intelligence that refuses betrayal.

The third is the *freedom of speech*—not the license to wound, but the courage to tell the truth when truth is unwelcome. To trust dialogue over destruction, because conversation is the most beautiful alternative to war.

The fourth is the *freedom of imagination*—to see beyond inevitability, beyond borders and binaries. To envision what has not yet been lived, to let the mind become a frontier of possibility—because imagination is resistance against despair.

The fifth is the *freedom of compassion*—to recognize the vulnerable as our own reflection. To let mercy outweigh mockery, tenderness undo cruelty, and to practice sacred reciprocity: your suffering is never separate from mine.

The sixth is the *freedom from violence*—to dismantle the machinery of war, not with vengeance but with conscience. Because violence and war are the primitive reflexes of fear, the lowest rung of human possibility. *Nonviolence is not naïve—it is evolution.*

The seventh is the *freedom of solidarity*—to know that my dignity is inseparable from yours, that no one is free until all are free. This is *erotic ubuntu*: I am because you are, and together we become. Erotic not as possession or performance, but as the current of aliveness that makes existence a creative adventure. It is sovereignty joined with mutuality, the pulse of being fully oneself while opening to the other, the art of freedom practiced together. To live this way is to know that intimacy and solidarity are not opposites but the same fire—one that refuses both isolation and domination.

The eighth is the *freedom of play*—because a civilization without joy, laughter, or creation has already surrendered to *death-in-life*. Play is not frivolous; it is the renewal of spirit, the breath that keeps culture alive. After all, only the humorless confuse gravity with depth—and only the dead mistake pleasure for sin.

The ninth is the *freedom of truth*—to resist propaganda and illusion, to stand against the industrial manufacture of lies. *Truth is mindful intelligence in action*: seeing things as they are, without distortion, without denial.

And finally, the tenth: the *freedom of becoming*—the right to evolve, to transform, to refuse the prison of fixed identities. To shed skins, to grow wings, to live as a verb not a noun—because *mindfully becoming is the dharma of existence* itself.

As Wilde might have said: *only the timid die unfinished, for it is better to risk ruin in transformation than to wither safely into respectability.*

Those are my ten. But may I invite you to craft your own ten, and inscribe them on the sacred walls of your heart and mind. *Your own politics of the heart.*

Live them, evolve them, let them breathe. Make them so honest, so deep, so lived, that they become the oxygen of your conscience and the aurora of your dignity—the vows that guide you past self-betrayal into the freedom of being *fully* alive.

And yes, I know—I risk cliché by using that word *fully* again. But far better to risk a cliché than to live one. After all, half-alive saints are only martyrs to mediocrity. And enlightenment, let's be clear, is not another five-star amenity—though on Maui, some of you may still try ordering it with room service... *with a side of ayahuasca.*

The Experiment of Freedom

Every age invents its own chains, and every generation must decide whether freedom is still worth the risk.

Let us bring it home—*here, now.* I love America—not the brand, not the empire, but the experiment: *the audacious wager that a people could live free.* And as I said earlier, I love the scandal of the First Amendment—the audacity to declare that every voice, every dissent, every disruptive word belongs in the public square. Speech is sacred. Dangerous. Untamable.

But do we still love it? Do you? Or have we begun to betray ourselves—trading liberty for algorithmically engineered indignation, monetized resentment, rehearsed prejudice, and a thousand masks of mockery parading as freedom?

Even in our so-called enlightened circles, we practice our own small treasons—gossip dressed up as discernment, the delicious collusion of lowering someone's status when they're not in the room. A *Burning Man* of betrayal—spiritual, psychological, exquisitely sophisticated—yet betrayal all the same.

Under the glow of the *Machine,* betrayal mutates: liberty is no longer argued over but anesthetized, exchanged for its scripts, its cages, its counterfeit choices. This is not freedom lost in a single act—it is freedom quietly smothered by design. That, my friends, is the question. *Will America still dare to be the laboratory of freedom—or will it outsource its conscience to the Machine?*

Because if Wilde was right—and disobedience is our original virtue—then the most radical rebellion left is to refuse obedience itself: to stand unscripted, unfiltered, disruptive—risking conscious chaos in pursuit of truth.

And if that sounds absurd, I'll let Wilde have the last word: *"If you want to tell people the truth, make them laugh, otherwise they'll kill you."*

So let me test that theory. Imagine this: what if we made a collective vow—like a sacred, irreverent, cosmic pinky-swear—to cease all negative talk? No more slicing reputations with tongue-knives, no more character assassinations in yoga studios or greenrooms. A vow so radical that we'd refuse to speak about anyone not present—unless, of course, it was Christ, Allah, Vishnu, Buddha, Trump, or the Devil. Those six have permanent hall passes. They've been trending for two millennia—they can take the heat.

Picture it: gossip dies overnight, cancel culture collapses from exhaustion, and the global economy—half of which runs on backbiting and "did you hear about...?"—goes into *freefall.* Entire industries vanish: tabloids, mainstream media, half of Hollywood. Even the self-help gurus go quiet—because, let's be real, if they can't tell you what's wrong with someone else, what's left to sell?

And maybe—just maybe—we'd rediscover what it's like to stand in someone's presence without weaponizing their absence. Imagine the awkward pauses, the pregnant silences. Imagine having to talk about weather, love, stars, sex, poetry, art, dogs, the galaxies—intimacy itself. Imagine actually feeling the miracle of each other, instead of chewing on reputations like spiritual beef jerky.

It would be chaos. Holy, hilarious chaos. And maybe that's what liberation looks like—*losing the taste for betrayal,* even the artisanal kind we pass around at festivals of self-congratulation.

So, let's talk—honestly, dangerously, joyfully. Let's make tonight a rainbow against the noise. Because not all silence is betrayal: some silence is sacred, a cathedral for the soul. But the silence that colludes with cruelty, that averts its eyes, that swallows the scream—that silence is unforgivable. And I refuse to commit it. Come with me.

The Final Betrayal

And yes, I am a sacredly celibate *trans-Buddhist*—fluid, feral, irreverent. Not rejecting, not renouncing, but refusing the coffin of any orthodoxy. Because the moment *Dharma*—the living principle of awakening— ossifies into doctrine, freedom gasps for air like a fish on the floor.

And if you must label it, call it this: *sapiosexual celibacy*—the heartful art of being erotically aroused by consciousness liberating itself from its own delusions. The slow undressing of ignorance through dialogue; the foreplay of eyes, mannerisms, and ideas; the body made luminous by thought; the mind expanding toward new horizons—without neglecting the earth beneath our feet or the air we breathe. In other words: desire, sublimated—not suppressed—transfigured into curiosity so alive it hums like felt music beneath the skin.

And clearly, freedom is not a brand. Not a slogan. Not a logo. Freedom is elemental—like breath, fire, love. It belongs to no one, and to everyone. Try to bottle it, codify it, weaponize it— and freedom doesn't just suffocate; it rots into perfume for tyrants.

So let us be clear: freedom is not obedience disguised as belonging, nor rebellion franchised by tech-bros and mega-influencers. Freedom is unboxed—messy, inconvenient, dangerous, alive; sometimes stoned, sometimes holy—but always its own wild animal: elemental, untamed, a sacred neuroplasticity radiant in creative purity. *A politics of the heart.*

And if it involves others, let it be with consent. You do not go before the United Nations to plead that genocide or that mass murder is better—that such slaughter is a necessary "clearance operation" or the tragic price of so-called democracy. That is not strategy; it is confession. Live your dream, yes—but never at the cost of another's dignity. And by no means factory-farm human beings for political survival or perverse pleasure.

That, my friends, is the final betrayal: when liberation becomes lifestyle, when conscience becomes content. Freedom without conscience is not freedom—it is domination. And freedom without love is not freedom—it is empire in drag.

Or, as Wilde might have whispered after too much absinthe: *some people bring happiness wherever they go; others, thank God, whenever they go.* And I'd add—freedom knows the difference. The question is: which one are you?

So here we stand—half digital, half divine—learning again how to touch without possession, how to meet without performing, how to love without consuming. To risk tenderness as rebellion, presence as protest. To practice the only revolution that endures: the disobedience of consensual, mutual intimacy—*eroticized ubuntu*, radiant with psychedelic luminosity.

Section II:
Burning Love in
the Time of Genocide

❉

The Cemetery of Borders

My dear friend Robert Chartoff—celebrated producer of forty-three films, including *The Right Stuff, New York, New York*, and the *Rocky* series—once invited me to script a feature film of my choice. When he asked what story, I wanted to tell, I said: *Love in the Time of Genocide*. It felt at once sacred and tragic, a title less like an idea and more like a vow—something that demanded not just to be written, but to be lived. That decision carried me to Zagreb, Croatia, where I was based during the final year of the Yugoslav wars.

It was the early-1990s. A conflict, a three-way convulsion of neighbors raged between Bosnian Muslims, Orthodox Serbs, and Catholic Croats—neighbors who had once lived, worked, and married across lines that suddenly hardened into trenches. Nationalism metastasized into madness; neighbors became targets. The map of Europe was being torn apart, borders redrawn not in ink but in blood.

Sarajevo had endured nearly four years under siege—the longest in modern warfare—its people encircled by tanks and snipers, cut off from food, water, and medicine. I did not enter the city until a few months after the Dayton Peace Accords ended the horror, when the guns finally fell silent. By then, an estimated 100,000 people had been killed—men, women, and children—and more than 2 million displaced—the worst bloodshed in Europe since World War II.

One afternoon, I walked through a hillside cemetery above the city with a new friend who wished to introduce me to her parents, buried there. As we moved among the stones, she spoke softly, almost matter-of-fact, about the ground we were crossing. What struck me first was not the silence but the order—the meticulous organization of death. *White marble for Muslims. Black for Catholics. Gray for Orthodox.* Even in death, the tribes could not be reconciled. Husbands and wives torn apart again, families consigned to eternal exile, divided by stone.

And I remember standing there, among those headstones, feeling the grotesque absurdity press down on me. This was war's final insult: *not only the slaughter of the body, but the partitioning of the soul.* Hatred carried beyond life, carved in stone, maintained for eternity. A cemetery turned into propaganda.

And I thought: this is not history's aberration—it is its blueprint.

We see it again today. In Gaza, families are erased before they reach the graveyard. In Ukraine, mass burials under frozen earth divide the dead into "ours" and "theirs." In Myanmar, students are executed, infants burned alive, whole villages obliterated—not merely for faith, but because a dictatorship, crazed by its militarized paranoia, feeds on fear. Its generals idolize cruelty, dividing majority from minority, as though domination were redemption.

Different uniforms. Different gods. The same disease: *power addicted to itself*, hallucinating eternity while annihilating freedom.

The Mass Grave

A few days earlier, I had driven through eastern Bosnia, near a town now synonymous with atrocity: Srebrenica. In July 1995, more than eight thousand Bosnian Muslim men and boys were executed in cold blood—fathers, sons, brothers lined up, shot, dumped into pits. The world was watching. The UN was present. Still, it happened.

But this wasn't anything new. History has always been littered with the same convulsions of ethnocentrism, xenophobia, and nationalism. The twentieth century wrote its scripture of blood—Stalin, the Holocaust, Hiroshima, the genocides in Timor and Rwanda, Pinochet's terror in Chile, Pol Pot's sea of skulls in Cambodia, the death squads of Guatemala, Saddam's massacre of the Kurds, the crushing of democracy in Burma, Tiananmen Square, the hanging of Ken Saro-Wiwa in Nigeria.

And now the blood continues. The razed neighborhoods of Aleppo. The endless funeral processions in Gaza. Bucha's frozen corpses in Ukraine. Darfur—again—where famine and fire stalk the land. The Uyghurs in Xinjiang, stripped of language, faith, and breath. The machinery of annihilation never sleeps; it only rebrands itself and relocates each decade.

Even in America we carry our own pits—lynching trees, Tulsa's ashes, classrooms turned into crime scenes. Our memory remains the unfinished trial of our conscience.

In the name of what—truth, freedom, nationalism, globalization, Christ, Allah, oil, God?

That day, after hours of driving through bombed-out villages, I stopped by the roadside. In a nearby field, some men were digging. I walked over. There it was—a mass grave. A pit of decomposing bodies. The stench was so overwhelming I gasped, covering my mouth, but the air itself was contaminated. It clung to the lungs, to the skin, as if the dead were demanding to be remembered.

I looked closer and saw a hand protruding from the soil. On its finger, a wedding ring—glinting in the sunlight like defiance itself. Was it a man or a woman? Muslim or Christian? Soldier or civilian? Impossible to know. All the labels had rotted away. Only the ring remained, testifying to love.

And suddenly I felt the collision of the paradox: here, in a graveyard of annihilation, the most ordinary human bond shone with transcendent radiance. *The ring declared: I am more than your hatred. I loved. I belonged. I promised. And though flesh is crushed, the vow endures.*

Even here, in genocide's abyss, love outlived hate.

And I knew: this was not Bosnia alone. This was *everywhere*.

The hand in Gaza, pulled from rubble. The hand in Ukraine, frozen beneath collapsed concrete. The hand in Myanmar, reaching from the ashes of a torched village. The hand in Sudan, clutching a ring as famine swallows the body. The hand in Xinjiang, silenced behind barbed wire. The hand in Haiti, reaching from collapsed schools amid violence and neglect. The hand in Congo, buried in a mine for cobalt that powers our devices. The hand in Yemen, brittle with hunger as bombs fall from foreign skies.

Everywhere, the hand remains—the unrelenting witness.

The grave says: you do not matter.

The hand says: I loved. I belonged. Remember me.

This is the architecture of atrocity: not just to kill the living, but to annihilate memory to strip a human of their story, to reduce them to waste.

And yet the ring gleams as testimony: that we are more than flags or tribes, and that something sacred survives every attempt at erasure.

The *Dharma* of Humanness

Standing there, staring at that ring, I realized something that cut deeper than any meditation ever had. For decades I had pursued transcendence, escape from duality, freedom from *samsara*. But in front of that pit, transcendence felt obscene —*a bypass masquerading as stillness.*

The *Dharma*, I saw, is not about leaving humanness but entering it—fully. Not about fleeing the world, but holding it. True liberation is not the end of suffering but the refusal to abandon compassion, even in hell.

As Jung warned us: *"The unlived life curdles into bitterness, rigidity, contempt."* And here was its ultimate expression—an unlived humanity congealed into genocide. People so divorced from their own inner life that they mutilated the lives of others.

As noted earlier, it was Oscar Wilde, with his lethal wit, who once said: *"If you want to tell people the truth, make them laugh, otherwise they'll kill you."* But there, at that pit, I realized the opposite was also true: the moment we forget to laugh, to love, to live, we begin to betray—and perhaps even to kill—not only others, but everything human within ourselves.

And so, I asked myself: what kind of consciousness would it take to use our hands not to harm, but to heal? Not to bury, but to bless? To entwine fingers in kindness instead of cruelty? Is this naïve idealism—or the only revolution left?

The Hands That Save Us: Auschwitz to Sarajevo
Several hundred miles from Sarajevo, just a few short years before, there was another graveyard of humanity—Auschwitz. *Have we learned nothing?*

I once heard the story of Yankel, a Jewish baker in Crown Heights who had survived the camps. He told it simply:

"I was a teenager when they put us in a boxcar headed for Auschwitz. It was night, freezing, the kind of cold that kills. The Germans left the cars on the tracks for days—no food, no blankets, no mercy. Next to me was an old man I knew from my town. He was shivering so violently I thought he would die before morning. I wrapped my arms around him. I rubbed his shoulders, his arms, his legs, his face. I begged him to hold on. All night long I rubbed, though my own hands were numb and I was sure I would not make it myself.

"Morning came. The sun rose. I looked around. Everyone else in that boxcar had frozen to death. The old man survived because someone kept him warm. And I survived because I was keeping him warm."

That is the lesson. Not theory, not ideology. *A hand refusing cruelty, choosing care. The power of touch to keep life alive in a world organized for death.*

And standing in the cemetery of Sarajevo, with its segregated stones—white for Muslims, black for Catholics, gray for Orthodox—I could not help but think: *the same hand that kills can warm, the same hand that buries can bless.*

And the question roars: *have we learned anything?*

Hands of Mercy: Sarajevo and the Last Revolution

The next day, the question followed me into a small clinic on the outskirts of Sarajevo. The rooms were heavy with trauma—some patients speechless, others sobbing uncontrollably.

And then I saw him: a boy no older than nine, clutching a teddy bear as if it were the last fragment of safety in a demolished world. His mother sat beside him, dabbing his tears with a handkerchief, and then her own. My friend, a doctor, lifted the sheet covering his body. Beneath it—nothing. No legs. She covered him again, gently kissed his cheek, whispered words of comfort.

I excused myself, overwhelmed, and walked outside. The question roared back: *what will it take for our hands to remember their purpose*—not to break, but to bless? Not to mutilate, but to mend? Not to weaponize, but to caress?

And I knew then: this is not sentiment—it is survival. This is the only revolution that has ever mattered, and the only one left.

Dostoevsky, that haunted genius of the Russian soul, warned us where the true battlefield lies: *"Beauty is mysterious as well as terrible. God and the devil are fighting there, and the battlefield is the human heart."*

And so, I turn to Václav Havel, who knew the machinery of dictatorship from the inside, and yet dared to speak of conscience, of tenderness, of responsibility. He told us, *"Without a global revolution in the sphere of human consciousness, nothing will change for the better in the sphere of our Being as humans."*

This, then, is the call: not just to resist tyrants "out there," but to confront the tyrant within—the small cruelties, the betrayals, the temptations to mock, to numb, to turn away. *The rehumanization of the spirit begins here, in the human heart, or it begins nowhere at all.*

So let us pause. Let us breathe. Let us dare to feel what history has begged us to feel: that every genocide, every dictatorship, every atrocity is not only "theirs," it is also ours—the same potential for cruelty, the same capacity for complicity, the same silence that becomes permission.

And yet—so too, the same capacity for mercy, for beauty, for a revolution of conscience that no army, no algorithm, no empire has ever managed to extinguish.

That, my friends, is why we are here tonight. Not to escape, but to enter. Not to bypass, but to embody. To remember together that the real war is not nation against nation, but spirit against betrayal. *A politics of the heart.*

And I thank you—for daring to go on this journey with me. And I invite you—let us go deeper tonight.

Section III:
The Politics of Pretending
Mockery, Denial, and the Death of Sovereignty

❄

The Empire of Pretend

We live in an age of pretending. It has become our shared religion, the oxygen of politics, the creed of culture, the altar at which the modern world kneels—burning incense to appearances.

Politicians pretend to represent the people while serving corporations. Corporations pretend to care for the planet while strip-mining it. Citizens perform awareness—while doomscrolling a choreography of rage; mistaking agitation for insight, and noise for truth. Nations pretend to uphold freedom while manufacturing prisons of the mind.

The theatre of pretending is vast. And its actors? Everyone with a pulse and a password.

We pretend our leaders are leaders while they celebrate domination. We pretend our votes are sacred while money buys every outcome. We pretend our borders are real while satellites mock at our lines. We pretend our wars are noble while bombs obliterate city blocks—and every living being within them. We pretend our gods are universal while sanctifying slaughter as prayer. We act like denizens of hell pretending to uphold the moral high ground. Kill. Kill, kill. *"A nasty job, but it must be done."*

We are, as Hannah Arendt warned, living through *the banality of evil*—not the spectacular violence alone, but the quiet normalization of hypocrisy. Evil no longer storms the gates; *it scrolls our feeds simultaneous to the scorching of villages.*

Pretending has become both the creed and the currency of survival. But every act of pretending is an act of self-betrayal. Every unspoken truth corrodes. Every mimicry of belonging fractures the soul.

And yet—why do we do it? Why do we keep pretending? Because it feels safer. Because truth is dangerous. Because reality threatens our comfort. Because the mask, at least, fits.

But here's the paradox: the more we pretend, the less safe we become. For in pretending, we collude with tyranny. We numb conscience. We surrender to the script. Pretending is the fentanyl of morality.

Pretending is not harmless. It is lethal. It is how genocides are allowed. How dictatorships endure. How democracies rot. Not with tanks at the gates alone, but with collusion at the dinner table, with laughter at the wrong jokes, with obedience to the script we know is false.

This is why Václav Havel, from inside a Czech prison cell, insisted: *"Living in truth is the power of the powerless."* Living in truth is not an idea; it is a refusal. *A refusal to participate in the theatre of lies.*

And that is why we are here tonight—to practice that refusal, together. For every time you speak the truth when silence is safer, you interrupt the theatre. Every time you refuse to mock what is sacred, you disrupt the script. Every time you stand up, even trembling, you fracture the stage on which tyrants depend.

The politics of pretending collapses not with revolutions alone, but with a single act of unmasking. The curtain falls the moment we stop performing.

And beneath all pretending lies its root: *denial.* For every theatre of illusion begins with the refusal to feel what we already know.

Denial: The First Betrayal

Denial is not ignorance. It is *refusal*—the first betrayal that makes pretending possible. It is the willful refusal to feel what is already evident. Denial is the narcotic of our age.

We deny grief. We deny fear. We deny the questions that erupt like fire in the night. And that refusal is not neutral. Denial is complicity. It saves the tyrant the trouble of censorship; we volunteer to censor ourselves. We *ghost* our own conscience.

But denial is unstable. It ferments. It calcifies into self-deception. And soon we no longer know where the mask ends—and the face begins.

And once you forget your own face, you will believe anyone's lie.

Self-Deception: The Glue of Propaganda

Self-deception is survival turned parasitic. We tell ourselves we are free while chained. We whisper we are safe as we suffocate. We insist we are good people even as our silence oils the gears of atrocity. Evil doesn't begin with monsters—it begins with employees.

Orwell called it *doublethink.* Jung called it *the split self.* Václav Havel called it *living in lies.* My Burmese teachers called it *moha*—self-delusion— the most dangerous of all poisons.

Propaganda wears the will thin; advertising dresses longing in satin and sells it back as salvation—rebranded as "fulfillment," neatly packaged and priced. One erodes refusal through exhaustion; the other invents appetite and peddles the lie that buying equals being.

The modern tyrant needs both—exhaustion as consent and false joy as a voluntary cage—yet the cruelest deception is domestic: the most dangerous lie is not the one told by dictators; it is the one we whisper into our own souls. Self-deception plants the first small denial; habit nurses it; law embalms it; empire grows in its shade.

Mockery: The Scalpel of Tyranny

Here's the trick every autocrat knows: laughter can kill conscience. Mockery is their scalpel. They ridicule the dead. They sneer at dissidents. They turn prophets into punchlines and martyrs into memes. And when the joke lands, civility takes the fall. When institutions bend—networks, owners, politicians—the joke graduates into policy.

But don't flatten the fact: we do their work for them. We mock the people who care too much; we lampoon our own outrage; we turn tenderness into theatre. That's how tyranny colonizes the psyche: not only with guns, but with ridicule. Mockery makes apathy fashionable; it turns compassion into comedy, sincerity into naïveté, truth into derangement. When caring becomes a punchline, who dares to rise?

And yet—the other edge: mockery can expose power's absurdities. Satire has toppled pretenders and exposed cruelty. The difference is intent and structure: who laughs, who funds the laugh, who amplifies it, who disciplines dissent afterwards. When the machinery behind the mock is the state, the corporation, or the media cartel, laughter becomes state-sanctioned anesthesia.

Which brings us to the darker twin: shame. Mockery cracks the armor; shame cements the cage. Ridicule opens the wound; shame teaches us to hide it. Together they chloroform the conscience, lulling rebellion into sleep.

Shame: The Lock on the Cage

If mockery is the scalpel, shame is the lock. Nothing freezes dissent like the fear of humiliation. Better to play along. Better to wear the mask. Better to pretend.

Dictators don't need to jail everyone. They only need to convince us that thinking differently is shameful, that speaking truth is madness. So, we become our own jailers—gagging our mouths, exiling our conscience. We stop needing censors; we become them.

That is the economy of self-betrayal: *the endless trade of dignity for belonging,* of truth for comfort. And shame is the currency. But every currency eventually collapses when the soul refuses to trade.

Mindful Intelligence: The End of Pretend

And yet, even now, there is a crack in the wall of illusion. A single pause— and in that pause lies the seed of freedom. That pause is everything: a slowing at the sense-doors—the eyes, the ears, the tongue, the nose, the skin, and the mind—where raw sensation arrives before the story begins. Between propaganda and belief lies sovereignty. Between mockery and shame lies freedom.

Sayadaw U Pandita once told me, "*Alan—do not vilify, but do not lie— especially to yourself.*"

That, to me, is *mindful intelligence.* The courage to see without distortion. The tenderness to understand without excuse. The refusal to be rushed into belief. The audacity to say: "*I will not play along.*"

Mindful intelligence does not live only in the head; it situates itself as a felt presence—a feeling-entity that scans the field. It listens to the timbre of mood, senses the frequency of an impulse, and reads the color of thoughts before they harden into conviction. It knows the grammar of *papañca*—the mind's cinematic habit of stitching sensation into story—and it learns to watch the projector rather than be hypnotized by the film.

Mindful intelligence is not theory; it is human survival. It is the moment you drop the mask—the instant you reclaim authorship of your own mind. It is the simple act of pausing before you swallow the script. It is the practiced noticing at the sense-doors: naming the image, hearing the tone, feeling the contraction in the belly, and asking whether this impulse consecrates life or desecrates it. The radical act of noticing, of choosing clarity over comfort. Here, pretending ends.

Here freedom quietly begins—without permission, without applause.

The Revolution of the Spirit

And so, it begins. Not in the ballot box, not in the battlefield, but in the psyche. In *the refusal to make-believe.*

Dictatorships collapse when people stop playing along. Democracies thrive when truth is spoken aloud. The *Dharma* is nothing less than the practice of reality itself. *And war—war is the endgame of pretense, the final act of betrayal against life.*

To live is not to pretend. To live is to awaken. And to awaken—let me tell you—is the most dangerous act in a culture addicted to illusion. Awakening is the only crime tyrants still fear.

That is the revolution of the spirit. That is *the insurrection of conscience.* And it begins with the simplest, most radical act of all: *dropping the mask.* Saying—with both fire and tenderness—enough.

Enough of the theatre. Enough of the pretending. Enough of the polite apocalypse.

Section IV:
A Literary Feature Film for the Conscience

When a Book Becomes Life—A Refusal to Betray Art & Conscience

✷

What could I do with this weight of knowing? The boy in Sarajevo became every child of every place where democracy is erased and dissidents disappear. The hand rising from the grave, the ring glistening in the sun—a gesture of defiance against annihilation, the stubborn pulse of freedom itself. I could not —*would not*— turn away.

I stayed with the struggle until a calling became clear: *art as defiance— imagination as survival.* The only rebellion left was creation itself—art as conscience, art as a love letter to my family in Myanmar. As Ai Weiwei said, *"Everything is art. Everything is politics."* To create was to breathe again—to transmute despair into witness, to bear truth into form.

Art as Insurgency

After nearly a year, I completed a 492-page illustrated novel, *Conversation with a Dictator: A Challenge to the Authoritarian Assault.* I never thought of it as a book. I wrote it as resistance—as requiem and rebellion. A refusal of complicity, of paralysis, of forgetting.

One reader called it *"A fusion of theatrical incantation and political art, with haunting black-and-white images that lay bare dictatorship's psychic wreckage."*

Another described it as *"a literary feature film staged inside the unconscious of a dictator—part testimony, part dialogue, part psychedelic séance."*

For me, it was a small act of nonviolent insurrection—an offering for my beloved Burma, and to every place where truth is forbidden.

Born from Defiance

This work rises from what was erased. After the 2021 military coup in Myanmar, the democratically elected leaders were imprisoned. Aung San Suu Kyi was disappeared into solitary confinement: no press, no letters, no photographs. Not even her son had heard from her. The generals did not only jail her body; they sought to obliterate her presence and her radiance.

So, I asked: what can one voice do against dictatorship?

My answer was to shape *Conversation with a Dictator* as *a theatre of conscience—a cinematic scripture of resistance, a literary feature film for the soul.* Five acts: confession, delusion, memory, reckoning, redemption. A confrontation between truth and power, between conscience and denial—a drama that could just as well be a dictator interrogating his own shadow in his final hour. Every page became a stripping away of masks, an invitation to look tyranny in the eye and not flinch.

When tyrants erase, art must remember. When power silences, imagination must resurrect. When the world forgets, creation must testify. When conscience burns, art becomes its own fierce flame.

Images Against Amnesia

Dictatorship is not only political—it is psychological. It warps perception, hollows memory, makes cruelty mundane. That is why I turned to images: hundreds of stark illustrations—children in ash, cathedrals of delusion, prisons of the mind.

Aung San Suu Kyi appears often, wordlessly—lotus, shadow, presence. Silenced in body, yet sovereign in image. These drawings are not ornament. They are the book's second voice—ink turned witness, image turned indictment.

One reviewer called them *"a spectrum of the human condition: the circuitry of tyranny, the ruins of conscience, and the faint silhouettes of redemption."*

Each drawing is a meditation, a dirge, a defiance. Each one—a wound, a witness, a seed. A book not meant to rest on a shelf, but to be passed hand-to-hand. Smuggled. Gifted. Shared. Not to fight, but to feel. To awaken. To act.

Literature as Fire and Refuge

I return to this line—not from habit, but as a summons renewed: Jung warned that the most corrosive force in life is the unlived life, the betrayal of one's deepest possibility. This book was born as my refusal of that betrayal. Imagination became oxygen; creation, became survival.

It insists on the stubborn possibility that even tyranny is not immune to remorse—that even the most brutal heart might yet be pierced by grief and turned toward humanity.

This is literature as insurgency—a nonviolent weapon, a mirror held to tyranny, a reminder that art, at its most dangerous, is also at its most sacred. Like the *Dharma*, it is both fire and refuge—illumination and shelter.

And since global freedom, peaceful coexistence, and the liberation of Myanmar—my second birthright—are at stake, remaining mute in what may be Myanmar's final hour would be to conspire with darkness.

The Commerce of Death

We must divorce weapons from profit. As long as fear remains a business model, war will be inevitable. The global arms trade is not an abstract ledger; it is a marketplace of annihilation with showrooms, quarterly reports, glossy brochures, and sales teams that smile across the tables where decisions are made.

The global arms trade—measured in trillions—markets annihilation as aspiration. Missiles are pitched like luxury cars; cluster bombs get product lines; the brochure photographs children playing in front of new "security" fences as if safety were a lifestyle brand. The machinery of war erases memory and monetizes despair.

Follow the money and you follow the anatomy of complicity: defense contractors list on stock exchanges; pension funds pick them for steady dividends; banks underwrite the deals; lobbyists brush shoulders with ministers; insurers calculate risk as if human bodies were actuarial abstractions.

Every factory that clamps a warhead to a fuselage is powered by ordinary hours clocked by ordinary people paid in ordinary wages— until those wages are laundered into the *ledger of slaughter*.

Supply chains run through friendly states, shell companies, and the tax havens that worship secrecy as a commodity. AI and autonomy now turn distance into obedience: the drone learns to prefer a silhouette over a life; the algorithm learns to discount despair.

Against this, the work of conscience must remember, must feel, must resist, and must reimagine life itself. We must map the commerce: the PLCs, the boardrooms, the trade shows, the small towns whose economies are welded to factories of death, and the ministries that speak of "security" while counting profit margins.

For every missile built, a mind must awaken. For every bomb dropped, a poem must rise. For every spreadsheet that normalizes slaughter, a witness must read the names of the erased aloud—slowly, insistently— until those names are no longer ledger entries but people again.

And yet let us be honest: we do not live in the fantasy of instant miracles. We cannot unmake factories overnight, halt every shipment, or scrub every column of profit from the books. What we can do—and what will come to define us—is *refuse the small contracts of complicity*. Refuse the applause that counts as consent. Refuse the salary earned from engines of death. Refuse the polite quiet that converts horror into routine.

This is not naïve maximalism; it is disciplined refusal—an interior insurgency that says: *I will not be enlisted in the vocabulary of violence*. It is practical solidarity: map the money, divest where you can, fund reparative infrastructure, amplify witnesses, and demand that institutions answer for their ledgers.

And while the machines of war still turn, cultivate what will outlast them—theater, schools, hospitals, public memory—so that when the counting stops, the work of repair is already waiting.

The Sacred Possibility of Redemption

Peace will not be born of killing the so-called enemy. The only true path forward is *redemption*—the rising above ancient hatreds and modern enmities, the deliberate work of fostering in one another the resurrection of the soul.

That is precisely where Act Five of *Conversation with a Dictator: A Challenge to the Authoritarian Assault* points us. Redemption does not begin with new laws but with new hearts—with the sacred, humbling labor of remorse, confession, restitution, and repair.

It begins not with blame nor ideology but with felt attention—silence, stillness, and the courage to awaken to our *interbeing* through the doorway of conscience and unvarnished truth.

This book is where I've placed what I have—my passion, my skills, my voice. It is my way of standing with *Myanmar's revolution of the spirit*—not through rhetoric, but through reverence; not through condemnation, but through imagination; not for conquest, but for awakening. For conscience. For Burma. For the world. *A politics of the heart.*

Because redemption is not an ending—it is the slow arithmetic of repair: rebuilding schools, purifying rivers, restoring water systems, returning land titles, transforming poisoned rubble into gardens, and naming the dead—one by one—in every village and market. It is love returning through the ruins, rebuilding what violence forgot.

And yet redemption must also move inward. The outer work of restoration depends upon the inner work of transformation. At the heart of this labor is *a dharmically-infused politics of non-revenge*—a revolution that begins not in parliament or prison, but in the human heart.

It is the deep experiential study of *mindful intelligence*—the practice of discerning presence: seeing clearly before acting, transforming habit into creativity, fear into mutuality, and power into the safeguarding of peace.

It is the cultivation of wisdom—*paññā* in Pāli—the direct understanding of impermanence *(anicca)*, not-self *(anattā)*, and the unsatisfactory nature of clinging *(dukkha)*.

To truly see *anicca* is to understand that all things—power, fame, grief, and even nations—are in flux. Nothing endures untouched. In leadership, this insight humbles arrogance and softens control; it reminds us that the purpose of power is not possession but protection—to serve what inevitably changes with care and foresight.

To realize *anattā* is to see through the illusion of separateness—the "I" that dominates, hoards, or fears. In politics, this becomes the foundation of *sacred mutuality*—acting not from ego but from empathy. The wise leader knows that there is no true victory that leaves others diminished, no peace built upon another's subjugation.

To penetrate *dukkha* is to recognize the suffering born of clinging—to ideologies, to enemies, to self-image, to certainty itself. It teaches that liberation, even in governance, arises when we release the compulsions of control and instead govern through awareness, restraint, and compassion.

From this seeing arises the *ten pāramīs*—the most radiant perfections of the heart, through which wisdom matures into virtue, understanding ripens into action, and leadership becomes an act of compassion.

Dāna—generosity, the joy of giving without agenda.

Sīla—integrity, the restraint that preserves dignity.

Nekkhamma—renunciation, the freedom of letting go of excess and ego.

Paññā—wisdom, the clarity that perceives without distortion.

Viriya—energy, the courage to act with endurance and faith.

Khanti—patience, the quiet strength that refuses harm.

Sacca—truthfulness, speech and action aligned with conscience.
Adhiṭṭhāna—determination, the vow to persist for the good.
Mettā—loving-kindness, goodwill that embraces even one's adversaries.
Upekkhā—equanimity, the balance that sustains freedom amidst chaos.

Together, these form a living architecture of moral intelligence—
the Dhamma applied to the world—a *World Dharma* where leadership is no
longer domination, but stewardship; and politics, no longer the art of
control, but the practice of awakening.

Such politics refuses *the outmoded dominator mindset of patriarchy*—that
ancient reflex of fear disguised as strength—and calls instead for a
deep inherent mutuality: the recognition that liberation is relational,
that to heal a nation we must learn to perceive without hatred and act
without harm.

The Closing Gesture—The Courage to Begin Again

Redemption, in the end, is not ideology but intimacy—the reaching
across the distance we have created between ourselves and one another.
It is the moment we stop defending our pain and begin listening again;
when we look into the eyes of those we once called enemy and see, at
last, a reflection of our own bewilderment and longing to be whole.

To say I am sorry is not weakness—it is courage in its purest form. It
is the beginning of repair—not only of relationships, but of the human
spirit itself. When we bow to one another, when we admit the harm,
we have caused through fear, indifference, or pride, something ancient
begins to heal: the war within us.

From that stillness, forgiveness becomes possible, and from
forgiveness, a new form of strength—the strength to care again, to
protect what remains sacred, and to build a future that does not repeat
the violence of the past.

Let this be our quiet revolution: to meet in the middle, to hold hands
across our differences, to see one another without armor or ideology,
and to vow—simply, humbly—to be better people, for our friends, our
families, our communities, and for the fragile, radiant future of life itself.
A politics of the heart.

Section V:
Into the Fire of Freedom

**From Maui's Shores to Burma's Prisons
—The Making of a Witness**

❋

People often ask me: How did you get involved with Myanmar's struggle for freedom and democracy?

Decades ago, I came to Maui. Not for tourism. Not for leisure. I came to flee the machinery of madness.

The Vietnam War was raging. Helicopters thundered across the evening news. Body bags arrived daily on American television screens—a nation selling bombs and dreams in the same breath.

I could not breathe that air.

I fled. Slept on sand with my beloved, a tent pitched by the ocean. Took LSD. Swam with dolphins. Passed through visions of Hindu gods whose eyes opened within my own. Practiced yoga on the beach until breath and tide became one rhythm. And somewhere in that rapture, I fell in love—with a woman, with life, with the radical possibility that existence itself could be free.

The Ache Beneath Paradise

But at my core, I was depressed. Surrounded by heaven, hollowed by hunger. Laughing outwardly, aching within. The ocean sparkled, rainbows arched, plumeria scented the trade winds—*and yet the silence inside me felt like drowning.*

Not peace—but futility. Psychedelics had touched oneness, emptiness—but none of it pierced the wound. None of it answered the existential ache that whispered beneath ecstacy.

Beneath every vision rose the same question: *Why?*

Why does life exist at all?

Why suffering?

Why the dread that seeps into joy?

Why such staggering inequality—one body feasting, another starving, under the same sky?

No ideology worked. Not capitalism. Not communism. Not oneness. Not emptiness.

No belief, no doctrine, no bliss touched the pain.

I was left stripped, defenseless, face to face with the nakedness of being. And in that confrontation, *the heartache inside me outweighed the beauty around me.*

The Search for Context

So, I kept moving. A few years later—overland to India, searching for a framework vast enough to hold the oldest questions: Who am I? What is freedom? What is truth?

I spent night after night at the burning ghats in Benares, on the banks of the River Ganges—watching the endless fires consume the bodies of the dead. Impermanence made visible, twenty-four hours a day. Long lines of people waiting for their turn to be carried to India's holiest place, laid down on a pyre, and burnt.

What sermon could be greater?

Then months in Bodh Gaya, circling the Bodhi tree where the Buddha was said to have awakened. What did it mean—to be free of *dukkha*? To step beyond anger, greed, despair, ignorance? To walk outside the wheel of life itself?

Meanwhile, the staggering poverty of Calcutta rose up like a mirror I could not turn from. Children with hollow eyes circled us, hands outstretched, crying out with hunger. Dozens of them. And the question tore through me: *Why them and not me? Why this accident of birth? What separates us?*

The ache grew sharper with every step. The closer I looked, the more unbearable it became. And yet all I could do was close my eyes and turn inward—searching my own mind for a way to live without betraying what I had seen.

And so, Burma rose high on the horizon of my life. Out of that crucible of fire and hunger, Burma became my North Star—where the path of conscience and awakening converged.

The First Glimpse of Burma

And then—across the threshold, where geography dissolved into destiny.

I longed to stay. To practice full-time *vipassanā*—insight meditation—drawn by a small book that had fallen into my hands: *Satipaṭṭhāna: Practical Insight Meditation* by the Venerable Mahasi Sayadaw. Just pages really, but in them I sensed a map—not of belief, but of direct seeing. A manual for dismantling delusion, moment by moment.

I wanted that practice. I wanted to plunge into that mystery.

The Gate Closes

But dictatorship ruled the borders. I was told: a one-week visa only. Enough time to feel the air of Rangoon, to glimpse the monasteries, to bow before statues of the Buddha polished smooth by centuries of devotion—but not enough time to enter.

The doors of *Dhamma* stood open, but the gates of politics were slammed shut. The chains of tyranny clamped down not only on citizens, but even on strangers, on seekers. The message was clear: no one escapes the shadow of power, not even the pilgrim who comes with nothing but questions.

Drifting Again

So, I drifted throughout Asia—Sri Lanka, Ladakh, Nepal—then back to America. A short, desperate stint in Los Angeles—aspiring to be a filmmaker. Drowning again in neon and noise, in the same emptiness I thought I had left behind.

Opening the Door

And then came the thought: If I cannot stay in Burma, I will bring Burma to me. If dictatorship closed the gates there, I would open a door here. So, I invited the great Venerable Mahasi Sayadaw—whose book had lit the spark in me—to come to America, along with a small group of Burmese monks, to conduct two ten-day *vipassanā* retreats.

At the end of the retreats, I asked permission to ordain with him. He was clear—cautious, even. He told me there was no precedent, no assurance, no record of foreigners receiving extended visas to remain in Burma, except diplomats.

But he said: *we will try.*

The Ordination

And out of sheer necessity—out of a desperation deeper than ambition— they shaved my head and I ordained as a Buddhist monk in New York City. It was not a career move. Not a romantic experiment. It was survival. To save my life, I entered the robes.

The Exile That Became My Initiation

The very next day, I flew with them back across the world—first to

London, then onward to Thailand, and, miraculously, across the threshold into Burma.

And then, on the very last day of my seven-day permit, as a taxi idled outside to take me to the airport, a one-way ticket to Bangkok folded in my shoulder bag, a representative from the regime arrived at the monastery. He carried unexpected news: *my visa would be extended.*

In that moment, everything turned. The doors that had been sealed shut cracked open, if only a little, and the impossible became possible.

I crossed the brink and a monastery in Rangoon. And that is where the real work began: *the dismantling of illusion, the long unmaking of self.*

Detoxing the Self

Not from chemicals alone, but from an entire civilization. Ten thousand miles from home, I found myself both a prisoner of an existential war and, at times, a sacred guest in a celestial garden. I began detoxing from Los Angeles. From American excess and the endless excuses that kept me from myself. From sex, from whiskey, from cigarettes, from Percodan, and cocaine. From the compulsions I had baptized as freedom. From the self-hatred I had disguised as joy.

And from the most insidious betrayal of all: *the lies I told myself—and believed.*

The lie that achievement is the same as meaning.

The lie that money is the same as worth.

The lie that religion is the same as truth.

The lie that silence is the same as peace—when often it is cowardice in disguise.

And the most seductive betrayal of all: believing that betraying myself beautifully could pass for freedom.

The Monastery as Furnace

The monastery became my rehab. But it was not gentle. Mindfulness, unremitting. Mandatory silence. Mandatory celibacy. Two meals a day. No food after noon. Four hours of sleep. Eyes lowered. Voice stilled. Twenty hours of meditation—eight sittings, six walks, and every other posture treated as sacred opportunity.

There were no holidays. No weekends. No time off. No escape.

Every breath interrogated. Every thought dragged into the light. Every flicker of desire or fear—exposed.

The body became a laboratory. The mind, a furnace. The heart, a battlefield.

The Judas Effect

And here, as I said earlier, Jung's warning returns—not as something I once read in a book, not as a memory from decades ago, but as a reality alive now. He named it the deepest corruption in life: *self-betrayal—the Judas effect within the human psyche*, that quiet, imperceptible turning against ourselves.

Sit in silence long enough and you see it everywhere—inside me, inside you. *The thousand small treasons by which we abandon ourselves*: the compromises, the lies, the self-sabotage we disguise as pleasure, as freedom, as survival.

The Court of Conscience

To sit still is to enter the tribunal of one's own heart—*to be humbled, or perish*. No hiding. No escape into intoxication, distraction, ideology. Only an unflinching confrontation with the ways we have deflected our own deepest possibility.

The practice was relentless: include it, see it, know it, release it — *again and again, until the illusion cracked*.

And in the ruins, something new was born: *the face of the one I had spent a lifetime outrunning—myself. Unmasked. Raw. Naked. Terrified. And— astonishingly—beautiful.*

The Instinct for Freedom

Because in that encounter, I touched what I believe lives in all of us: *the instinct for freedom.* The natural urge of the human heart to know itself. Not a gift bestowed by governments or gods, but the marrow of our being. *An uncontrived naturalness*—as effortless as the breath, as inevitable as the tide. The metaphysical urge—the pulse that cracks the seed, that dissolves the caterpillar into imaginal cells, that ruptures the chrysalis into wings. *It is metamorphosis itself—the body of the universe aching to know itself as free.*

Freedom Remembered

This *instinct* is not ideology. It is not a slogan. It is not even a choice. It is the irrepressible current of life pushing through every vein, every silence, every scream. It can be delayed, distorted, betrayed. It can be imprisoned in a cell or crucified on the front page of history. But it cannot be erased.

For even when freedom is counterfeited—when comfort masquerades as courage, when conformity dresses as conscience, when silence pretends to be peace—the *instinct* endures. Sit still long enough and you will see it: the Judas effect, that quiet treason within, the thousand subtle ways we abandon ourselves, the compromises and self-sabotage we disguise as survival. Yet equally, you will glimpse *the holy unexpected—the heart's refusal to be deceived.*

The Dharma life is a daily reawakening—a cartography of mystery, mapping the sacred terrain of being. Turning our lives into an epic adventure, we blaze our own trails, even if it means defying social mores or breaking taboos that attempt to suppress and control our impulses.

This revolution will not be won or lost in a meditation retreat, a city street, a living room, or a monastery alone. It will happen on the front lines of the human heart—that stormy region where good and evil, genius and madness, peace and war battle for dominion over conscience, freedom, and love.

When compromise, doubt, or hesitation no longer appeal, you will catch a glimpse of the holy unexpected once more. You will begin listening to your instinct for freedom—to what you truly love—and leave the rest behind.

Part II:

CONSCIENCE

Section VI:
Dictators, Generals, and the Soul of Conscience

❋

Because if freedom lives or dies in the human heart, it also inevitably spills into history. The same treason we glimpse in silence—the Judas effect within—erupts upon the stage of nations: draped in medals, erecting prisons, orchestrating purges, baptizing whole civilizations in blood beneath banners of destiny.

From Solitary Confinement to the Killing Fields

And so it was in Burma, where the front lines of the human heart became the fault lines of a nation. At the *Mahasi Sasana Yeiktha monastery*—called a charnel ground for *kilesa*, the defilements of mind—those twisted habits of consciousness that betray the self and ripen into suffering were laid bare. When left unchecked, they metastasize beyond the individual. They become dictatorships. Gulags. Killing fields.

It was there that I met a man who would change my life.

The former Supreme General of Burma's Army.

His name was U Tin Oo.

He had been imprisoned by the same dictator who had once—by bureaucratic accident or fate—granted my visa to remain in Burma. And why was he imprisoned? Not for corruption. Not for treason. But for the most dangerous quality of all in a dictatorship: *the capacity to be loved.*

U Tin Oo was beloved. Trusted. And so, Ne Win, Burma's long-reigning strong man, struck first—locking his senior general in solitary confinement for six years.

The Smuggled Book

Six years with nothing but his mind. No visitors. No voice but his own. And then, by chance—or perhaps something deeper—a single book was smuggled into his cell: *Satipaṭṭhāna: Practical Insight Meditation* by the Venerable Mahasi Sayadaw. The very same book that had fallen into my hands in 1971, a text that pulled me toward Burma like a compass pointing to true north.

The thought still startles me: a prisoner in solitary confinement and a young seeker half a world away, both holding the same slim volume, tracing the same instructions, guided by the same teacher we would one day share.

And what did that book teach? The same radical instruction traced back to the Buddha 2,600 years ago and carried forward by countless others: *the practice of pure seeing—to look directly, to face reality as it is, without distortion; to dismantle delusion, moment by moment—the antidote to self-betrayal.*

As Mahasi wrote: "Ignorance conceals the true nature of things, and mindfulness reveals it. From the insight gained, liberation from greed, fear, and ignorance unfolds. Thus, the most important thing one can do in a lifetime is to practice intensive insight *(vipassana)* meditation."

The day after his release from prison, U Tin Oo chose a different kind of freedom. Quietly, with friends and family beside him, he entered the monastery and ordained as a monk. No podium. No speech. Just robes. A shaved head. Silence. An act of surrender that resounded louder than any manifesto: the true battlefield is within.

That is the man I met. Twenty-four years my senior. A veteran of World War II. Commander-in-chief of the *Tatmadaw*, Burma's army. Known for his bravery. A survivor of hand-to-hand combat. A man who had lived inside the belly of dictatorship and returned, not with bitterness, but with something far rarer: a vow of peace. *A renunciation of violence in all its forms—a luminous act of redemption.*

The Psychology of Tyranny

Somehow, across the gulf of age and circumstance, he befriended me, and with patient, quiet clarity he revealed *the anatomy of tyranny—the psychology of dictatorship, the pathology of totalitarianism.*

He explained that it does not always erupt in sudden violence but seeps forward like gas—odorless, invisible—advancing inch by inch, sown in unrecognized authoritarian impulses, in habits buried deep within the psyche of each of us. It germinates in the allure of privilege, in the seduction of power, in the subtle whisper that tempts us to trade principle for comfort, integrity for influence, silence for survival.

But what struck me most was his demand for honesty—the unrelenting challenge, he said, to stand before the mirror of one's conscience without escape, to look directly, day after day, at what you have done, what you have colluded with, what you have ignored.

"I see their faces still," he confessed. "Men I killed in war. Others I ordered to kill. At the time I called it duty. I called it loyalty. But that duty was nothing more than obedience to lies—*Orwellian lies swallowed as truth—until the acid of self-honesty burned them away.*"

And then he explained what he meant. *Collusion is rarely dramatic.* It is not always signing decrees or loading rifles. More often it begins in silence: in wanting to belong, in nodding when you disagree, in following orthodoxy because it feels safer than standing alone, in swallowing indoctrination because everyone else is swallowing it too. Step by step, almost unnoticed, you surrender yourself—truth for approval, conscience for convenience, dignity for the illusion of safety. That is collusion: *the betrayal of yourself in order to fit in.*

And so, he insisted: *you must question.* Question again. Question even your questioning. Do not stop at what is fashionable or convenient. Probe it. Sense it in the body—listen for the flinch or the ease. Does it ring true? Does it carry the texture of conscience?

Then he spoke of what endures beyond ideology, beyond armies and dictatorships: *hiri* and *ottappa.* Moral shame and moral dread. Not the shame of being seen, nor the fear of punishment, but the inner intelligence of conscience itself.

Hiri is the sensitivity that recoils from doing harm. *Ottappa* is the clear-eyed dread that foresees the consequences of cruelty. Together, he said, they are the true protectors of the world. Without them, civilization collapses. With them, even in prison, a man can remain free.

One moment from that day has never left me. He fixed his eyes on mine and said: *"Be aware of collusion. The surrender of your conscience, your dignity, your voice—that is how they imprison you without walls."*

Freedom of Spirit

And what struck me most was not only his warning, but his being. There was no bitterness in him. No residue of resentment. Not even toward his comrades who had betrayed him, nor toward the dictator himself, whose treachery was epic.

His freedom was not of geography but of spirit. He told me, with quiet conviction: "That imprisonment, with that book, was the greatest gift of my life. Not only did I survive prison—I thrived. I practiced *Satipaṭṭhāna* every single day. Each breath became my freedom. Each moment, the chance to see clearly. That is how I overcame captivity—

not by resisting the bars, but by refusing to betray myself."

And here Jung's warning returned, not as theory but embodied before me: the deepest corruption in life is self-betrayal—that Judas effect within the human psyche, that quiet turning against ourselves.

U Tin Oo had lived its antidote. In the silence of his cell, he practiced what might be called the counter-betrayal: meeting each moment honestly, until what should have broken him became the ground of his strength. *A politics of the heart.*

The Mirror for Us All

That was his liberation. Not the absence of walls, but the refusal to collude with the lies that once imprisoned his heart.

And I tell you this not as history, not as biography, but as a mirror. Because U Tin Oo's cell is not far from us. Each of us lives inside a confinement of our own design—circumstances we did not choose, walls we may not even see. And yet, inside those walls, the same choice is alive: *betray ourselves, or see clearly.*

Satipaṭṭhāna—this radical act of pure seeing—is not exotic, not foreign, not reserved for nuns and monks in Burma. It is here. In this breath. In this body. In this moment. *The antidote to self-betrayal is available now.*

And perhaps that is the point. Dictators may win battles. They may build prisons. They may bury truth under propaganda and fear. But they cannot reach into the marrow of our being and steal our *instinct for freedom.* That belongs to us—our inheritance, our birthright, our treasure.

So, the question is not: whether tyranny will end? *The question is: do we betray ourselves, or dare to be free—even here, even now?*

Baptism by Fire

Years later, I went underground in the jungles of northern Burma. The 1988 uprising had been crushed—thousands of unarmed protesters slaughtered on the orders of the same dictator who once jailed U Tin Oo. The battlefield he had revealed to me from the depths of his heart in solitary confinement now stretched across the entire nation.

I had not stood in the streets to witness indoctrinated troops fire on their own people. But when I crossed the border soon after, slipping into the resistance, the air was still heavy with massacre.

The silence of charred villages was not peace—it was shock. Children whispered instead of laughed. Mothers carried eyes that no longer blinked. Men spoke in fragments, if at all.

In the north, I saw jets strafe bamboo huts. Bombs crater rice fields where only days before children had been playing. Rifles slung across the shoulders of boys barely old enough to shave. Drugs pouring across borders—financing militias, fueling terror, turning survival itself into a weapon.

I had never been in a war zone before. And yes—it was chilling. Triple-canopy jungle warfare, enemy combatants all around, no clear line of demarcation. Gunfire ripped overhead as we huddled in trenches through the night. The metallic taste of fear coated my mouth. The question in every moment: *Will I live through the night? Will I see the day?*

And yet—paradoxically—I was alive again. More alive than I had ever been in the safety of the West. Not enlightened. Not serene. But alive. Face-to-face with the unrelenting question: *what does nonviolence mean here?*

Because despite it all—within it, beneath it—the pulse of freedom had not been extinguished. It had been ignited. You could feel it—not as rumor, not as wishful thinking, but as something burning in the marrow of the people. This was the beginning of a revolution not only of politics, but of the spirit itself—the uprising of the human soul to radiate even in the ashes of collective trauma.

All We Want is Freedom

One evening, in that same jungle, I sat with a young Burmese woman—a twenty-nine-year-old university graduate who had fled after the massacres. A single candle flickered between us as the distant sound of students' guitars drifted through the trees. She told me, slowly, that she had once been in love.

She and her fiancé planned to marry in late 1988. But only months before the wedding, the uprisings began. First, she marched with her fiancé. Then her brothers and sisters joined. Then her parents. Then her uncles and aunts. "Suddenly," she said, "my whole family was in the streets." They knelt before soldiers, singing, *We love you, you are our brothers. All we want is freedom. All we want is democracy.*

The soldiers fired. She watched friends and family gunned down, one dying in her arms. She and her fiancé fled with other students into the jungle. For two weeks they ran—hiding under leaves, clinging to riverbanks, covering their mouths as soldiers passed within arm's reach. Malaria set in. Fever, nausea, exhaustion. And then one night, ambushed, she and her fiancé were torn apart in the chaos. She has not seen him since.

"I don't know if he is alive," she said. "I dare not contact his family, or even mine. It would put them in danger."

Her eyes glowed steady in the firelight. "Yes, I still love him," she whispered. "But my values have changed. *I am in love with freedom.* Even if I am caught, even if I am tortured to death, if it helps restore freedom to my country, I will die in love. Yes, I have been in love. And I remain in love."

Her vow was not sentimental—it was revolutionary. It was Srebrenica's wedding ring glinting in the grave—but here, in the Burmese jungle. A marriage beyond marriage—a vow to life itself, to freedom itself.

And I knew then that the revolution of Myanmar was not only political—it was spiritual. *A people married to conscience.*

You could feel that moral courage had been awakened, and there would be no turning back. Obstacles, yes. Brutality, yes. But the people's will would not be broken. It would rise like never before—uncontainable, undeniable.

And I felt it pierce into my own soul—not as an idea, not as solidarity from afar, but as a summons. Something alive, insistent, undeniable. The same summons that would years later become *Conversation with a Dictator.* I knew then: *I did not just want to witness it. I wanted to belong to it—to serve it—to embody it.*

The Question of Nonviolence

It is easy to speak of peace when you are safe, when your belly is full, when your borders are secure. But when bombs fall on villages? When soldiers torch homes with families still inside? When monks are dragged into trucks, never to be seen again? Then nonviolence is no longer philosophy—it becomes trial by fire.

In that jungle, I felt the collision of ideals and survival. Nonviolence was no longer abstract. No longer a teaching in a book or a discourse from a monk. It was a flame searing at the crossroads of conscience: resist with weapons, or resist with spirit? Pick up the gun—or the vow?

I watched young men wrestle with this question with their lives on the line. One clutching a rusted rifle, saying, "If I don't kill, they will kill my family." Another holding a worn Buddhist rosary, whispering, "If I kill, I lose the reason to live."

And I stood between them—trembling—knowing that in me, too, lived both voices. The impulse to strike back in rage. The calling to resist with compassion. Violence and nonviolence were no longer theories, but blood and bone—a civil war within the soul.

And in that moment, I saw more clearly than ever: the true battlefield was not Burma—it was the human heart.

Nonviolence, I learned, is not passivity; it is disciplined ferocity without hatred. *A politics of the heart.*

The Witness Emerges

And so, my journey did not end there. It began anew—with the writing of my first book: *Burma: The Next Killing Fields?* Born of that jungle, blessed with a foreword by His Holiness the Dalai Lama. Not reportage. Not detached journalism. But a cry. A testimony. A witness to what I had seen, what I had felt, what had torn through me.

It was my vow—etched in words—to never look away. And I tell you now: that vow is not mine alone. It belongs to us all. Because the battlefield I speak of—the clash between rage and compassion, vengeance and conscience—is not confined to Burma's jungles. It is alive in this very room. It is alive in you.

Each of us, every day, is asked: Do I betray myself—or dare to remain free? Do I collude with silence, with convenience, with fear? Or do I stand as witness, as conscience, as love refusing erasure?

Section VII:
The Trans-Political Mandala

The Art of Non-Self-Betrayal

✻

This is why the *Dharma* matters. This is why mindfulness matters—not as a lifestyle pacifier or a branded headspace, but as the uncompromising craft and discipline of liberating consciousness itself—from fear, shame, greed, self-loathing, and the ancient habit of dominating or diminishing.

As Sayadaw U Pandita, successor to the great Mahasi Sayadaw, often reminded us: It is not enough to know the *Dhamma*—*it must become our oxygen.*

Leadership, then, is not charisma in the spotlight or ideology on a banner. It is metamorphosis in the marrow, the quiet alchemy of self-mastery. Leadership is measured by inner clarity, restraint, compassion, and truth. For leadership without conscience decays into tyranny. Power without empathy congeals into terror. And intelligence without morality collapses into mere cunning.

And so, the word *"trans-political"* returns like a *mantra*, because to live by conscience—to bear witness authentically—demands that we step beyond the gladiator pit of left and right. Beyond the algorithmic hypnosis of "us" and "them." Beyond the mockery of freedom marketed as product, shredded into sound bites, reduced to tribes and tags.

In today's fractured landscape, trans-political is not ideology—it is initiation. It is a summons of conscience, *a living mandala of interbeing*—an embodied riddle that throbs like a pulse in the bone, a luminous landscape of mutual freedom. Beyond "you're right" and "I'm wrong." Beyond "I'm right" and "you're wrong." It is the raw recognition that we may both be right—and that our differences are not a threat but a gift.

To live trans-political is to cultivate the moral courage to descend deeper and the imagination to rise higher—until freedom itself ceases to be a position and becomes an atmosphere, a shared breath, a way of being and becoming—together, in sacred reciprocity—an *eroticized ubuntu.*

Together, we are called to lift freedom into another dimension—participating in culture, society, and democracy not as consumers of spectacle, but as co-authors of conscience itself. Refusing to collapse into egotism, narcissism—or the reflexive comfort of authority—or into the subtler betrayal of performance and pretense. Choosing instead the harder path: to craft a justice supple enough to hold paradox without nailing it to the cross of certainty, without crucifying it on the rack of dogma.

And the wisdom is plain, though difficult: freedom itself is transcendent—unfinished, resonant and trembling, yet radiant in its broken wholeness. A freedom that refuses borders, refuses labels, refuses capture. A freedom that moves like weather, like breath, like eros, like a poem tearing up its own last line and casting it into the sky—where it dissolves not into conclusion, but into constellation. A horizon of shared becoming, a democracy not of votes but of vision. And let us be clear: a freedom that is mutual, fearless, and inclusive—radiant with hope, peace, and the creative possibility of all beings.

And yet, let us be equally clear: this trans-political freedom demands that we disarm the subtle violences of the mind and heart—all poisons rooted in the ancient delusion of "I'm right, you're wrong, bang, you're dead." To confront these roots is to unseat tyranny at its psychological source—to awaken, once more, the shared breath of our humanity.

Beyond the Binary of Red and Blue

Left and right are twin mirrors, each reflecting the other's obsession with opposition. One cries "return," the other "advance," yet both remain captive to the gravity of ideology. The trans-political steps away from that weary axis, refusing the theatre of rivalry, and seeks freedom not in the scaffolding of systems or the dogma of parties, but in the sanctity of lived conscience—the uncolonized dignity of existence itself.

Trans-political doesn't mean apolitical; it means conscious engagement without captivity. You can, of course, remain embracing of your respective political affiliations. I'm simply suggesting that we, as freedom-loving people, place conscience, dignity, mutuality, and compassion before party allegiance—a rare act now, both in a nation and a divided world where policy has become sport and citizens become its spectators.

Worse still, we are fed forever wars—endless cycles of devastation and reconstruction—the choreography of desecration repeated as if memory itself were under occupation. Have we not yet learned that no ideology can redeem the suffering it manufactures?

Which brings us home to the axis of renewal—conscience and mindful intelligence—twin faculties of ethical awakening. Conscience is the interior art of discernment, the pulse of awareness that instinctively flinches at harm, the subtle symmetry between truth and tenderness. Mindful intelligence is its companion: the art of seeing clearly before reacting, of feeling the shape of harm before reason attempts to justify it. Together they form an operating system of intuitive wisdom, rooted in *hiri* and *ottappa*—those luminous guardians of self-respect and moral restraint.

By conscience, then, I do not mean ideology or belief, but *a mindful intimacy with truth* arising from the still center of being—the quiet spine of dignity itself. From that intimacy, a new kind of politics can be born—neither red nor blue, but human—animated by reverence, restraint, and *the refusal to dehumanize.*

The Still Point of Freedom

Here, at the still point of freedom, conscience transcends certainty and truth is felt rather than enforced. It is the quiet heart-center where politics dissolves into presence, where ideology yields to the luminous clarity of compassionate awareness itself.

It is also the lucid axis of intuitive discernment—that delicate interval between perception, speech, and action—where inner life becomes ethically refined through the repeated activation of mindful intelligence. In that space, being turns transparent—radiant with responsibility—and every gesture becomes a referendum on integrity, rooted in conscience, suffused with mutuality.

It is the celebration of shared freedom—where freedom of speech is not a weapon but a gift; where dialogue becomes an art of co-creation, a communion through difference—a fertile atmosphere in which ideas are tested with rigor and grace rather than shredded with derision. Here, conversation becomes contemplation, and disagreement becomes a doorway rather than a wall.

Here, societal transformation is nurtured not by coercion, hatred, or vilification, but by love of truth and reverence for language itself—its tonality, its intention—*the poetics of precision joined with the ethics of care, the syntax of sincerity joined with the music of empathy*—married to the oldest political wisdom of all: *basic human decency.*

For in the end, conscience is the invisible architecture of civilization—that silent crossing between self and other, power and mercy, justice and love. It is the one faculty that tyranny cannot counterfeit, the last freedom no authority can revoke. To live trans-politically is to inhabit that crossing—to walk it daily, vulnerable yet awake, reverent yet unafraid.

Dharma as Compass

In Buddhist thought, *Dhamma* is not dogma but the law of reality itself—impermanence, interdependence, compassion, awareness. To see through *Dhamma* is to see through illusion: to recognize that nothing stands alone, nothing lasts, and nothing thrives without care.

A trans-political vision is dharmic politics—*politics of awakening*: not loyalty to doctrine, but devotion to mindful inquiry. It asks, relentlessly: What reduces suffering? What dignifies life? What liberates conscience? These are not rhetorical questions but living koans —*guides* for the art of action and the poetry of restraint.

Here, mindfulness is not a tool for sensory precision alone, but *a feminine-embraced intuitive intelligence—a disciplined hypersensitivity to the vibrational consequence of every thought, word, and deed.* It is the wisdom of self-accountability, the quiet art of listening for the echo of one's own mind in the fabric of existence. Each impulse becomes an inquiry: does this uplift or diminish life, sow peace or seed fear, harmonize or divide?

In this way, mindfulness matures beyond technique into a moral artistry—the cultivation of presence that feels before it acts, that measures truth not by doctrine, but by the tenderness it leaves in its wake.

To hold *Dhamma* as compass is to cultivate skillfulness in thought, speech, and action. It is the artistry of intention, where the measure of politics is not victory over an enemy, but the widening of possibility, the deepening of trust, the flowering of conscience. It is the refusal to weaponize language into derision or hatred, and the determination to use *dialogue as a field of awakening.*

Dharmic politics is not ideology dressed in spiritual attire—it is conscience made luminous, the unyielding practice of humanity in action. It is the elevation of life itself, without exception, and the compassionate embrace of those yet unborn—the inheritors of all we choose to create or destroy.

From Identity to Universality

Labels fracture us—liberal, conservative, man, woman, East, West. But labels are skins, not marrow. Beneath them is the shared pulse: every being longs to be free, safe, loved. That is the real constituency. That is the true congress. As I shared earlier, in speaking of what I call *eroticized ubuntu*—let me return, briefly but more deeply.

By "erotic," I mean not sex, but the adventurous creativity of being alive—the refusal to reduce existence to transaction. It is eros in its oldest sense: the pulse of interconnection, the raw, generative energy of relation itself.

And *ubuntu*—a word from Southern Africa often rendered as *I am because we are*—is the wisdom that personhood is never private property, but shared inheritance. At its finest, *ubuntu* declares that dignity is indivisible, that the human self is only real in relation to others.

To *eroticize ubuntu*, then, is to bring to this principle not only ethics but imagination—to re-enchant our shared belonging, to feel the pulse of the same earth beneath our feet, the same air in our lungs, the same water that remembers us all. It is to know that your longing for freedom is not separate from mine; your dignity is woven into my own; your suffering diminishes my humanity, and your awakening enlarges it. *Human rights, in this light, are not parchment ideals but the living tissue of coexistence*—a sensual covenant of care, breathing through every act of recognition.

To live this way is to *discover one's own Dhamma aesthetic*—the unique rhythm of becoming through which transformation and freedom express themselves. No two awakenings move alike: each body, each mind, each heart improvises the art of liberation in its own tongue. The way we walk, smile, listen, or dance—these are not mere gestures but the choreography of consciousness itself. Freedom is not uniform; it improvises its way into being through authenticity, through the courage to love unguardedly, to create without permission, to belong without possession.

This is the erotic of *ubuntu*—where ethics and imagination entwine, where the boundaries between self and other soften into music, and the practice of freedom becomes *a shared art.*

The Art of Being Human Together

And the question becomes: *how do we live our lives together and apart?* How do we honor our differences—our languages, our cultures, our rituals— while knowing that the breath in your lungs and the breath in mine are drawn from the same atmosphere? This is the moral and existential imagination of *eroticized ubuntu*: a politics of the heart wide enough to embrace separation and intimacy, individuality and interdependence— without betrayal.

Picture it: a starving, traumatized child in Myanmar, cradled in the trembling arms of a parent who can do nothing but hold her. And three thousand miles away, a young girl in Bali, glowing with health, also embraced by her parents beneath an open sky. Different lives, different fates—and yet, in that gesture of embrace, something universal is revealed: the same ache for safety, the same tenderness of love, the same longing that no ideology, no border, no war can erase.

That is *eroticized ubuntu*—not sentimental, not abstract, but *embodied global empathy*: the recognition that Myanmar and Bali are not separate universes but mirrors; that the fate of one child, anywhere, is bound to the dignity of every child, everywhere. *Freedom is not yours or mine, but ours—or it is nothing at all.*

The Embodied Mandala of Freedom

To speak of the trans-political is no longer merely to think differently— it is to live as though freedom were breath itself, moving through sinew and speech, shaping the texture of daily life. To rise each morning knowing your choices inscribe the invisible, that every act leaves a trace upon the shared canvas of being.

This is not abstraction but practice—the quiet choreography of integrity. Each movement, each silence, each refusal to betray what you know to be true becomes part of a larger pattern unfolding through you.

To live *the mandala of freedom* is to let awareness compose the body's rhythm—to speak with clarity, to listen without defense, to meet difference with respect. It is to wear compassion like the skin of existence itself—tender, porous, alive.

And in this way, freedom ceases to be a destination or an entitlement; it becomes a living rhythm, a pulse of reciprocity, a shared art of breath and belonging. The mandala is never fixed—drawn and erased with each moment's mindfulness—until *the art of living becomes indistinguishable from the art of liberation.*

The Poetics of Mutual Becoming

Freedom, at its most intimate, is poetry incarnate—not the ornament of language but the living pulse of being. Prose is too narrow for its amplitude; dogma, too brittle for its tenderness; orthodoxy, too slow for its fire. Freedom is eros in motion, quivering yet unbroken, forever unfinished at its edges. It is the vow whispered before completion, the breath that resists punctuation, the half-spoken sentence that refuses to end because ending would mean closure, and closure would mean death.

To speak of mutual becoming is to recognize that the future is never possessed, only co-created. It is not my victory or your defeat, not the triumph of one will over another, but something subtler, stranger, and infinitely more beautiful: our interwoven flowering, our shared unfinishedness, the humility to evolve together without knowing the outcome.

Eroticized ubuntu, then, is not merely an ethical principle but a poetics of interbeing—a way of seeing the world as kin. It is to look upon the child in Myanmar and the child in Bali, the mother in Gaza and the father in Maui, not as symbols of tragedy or fortune but as mirrors of the same ache for safety, the same hunger for tenderness, the same unspoken plea to belong in a world that keeps forgetting its own heart. It is to know, with unflinching intimacy, that your freedom and mine are not parallel lines but converging currents, that every act of betrayal ripples outward to wound us all, and that to honor another's dignity is to secure the integrity of one's own.

Freedom, therefore, is not a noun but a verb conjugated by care—written in relationship, erased by indifference, and reborn each time courage leans again toward love. It is less a possession than a practice, less a theory than a rhythm of shared aliveness, the willingness to keep creating the world together, however broken it may be.

Dismantling Authoritarianism at Its Root

Authoritarianism thrives wherever rigidity replaces reflection—wherever the mind hardens into certainty and identity calcifies into weaponry. It feeds on fear, fattens on division, and mistakes control for coherence. It survives because we forget how to imagine otherwise.

The trans-political sensibility refuses this captivity. It does not announce its rebellion with slogans or flags; rather, it dissolves the architecture of domination quietly—through understanding, empathy, and the disciplined refusal to dehumanize. Its defiance is almost invisible: a soft vigilance that says, I will not be reduced; I will not let language become a cage.

In *dharmic* terms, this is non-attachment translated into civic life—belonging without bondage, caring without conquest, participating without being possessed by the momentum of ideology. It is the art of remaining in relationship without surrendering discernment, of engaging the world's suffering without being devoured by its rage.

To dismantle authoritarianism at its root is not only to confront its external machinery but to disarm its psychological infrastructure—the reflex of fear, the addiction to certainty disguised as truth, the subtle collusion between ego and obedience. True resistance is an interior revolution: to reclaim fluidity where power demands rigidity, to cultivate a freedom supple enough to hold contradiction without weaponizing it.

This, ultimately, is *Dhamma as politics*—not a creed but a compass, guiding us to meet the world with clarity that does not harden, conscience that does not retreat, and courage that does not need to roar.

The Sacred Task of Becoming

Democracy, in its most luminous sense, is not machinery, nor flag, nor law—it is a living meditation, a civic yoga of conscience practiced in the ordinary gestures of daily life. Freedom is not a destination but a discipline, the ceaseless art of awakening in relationship. The question, then, is not Who wins power? but How do we awaken together without leaving anyone behind?

Freedom is never static; it is becoming itself—the refinement of conscience, the dignity of reciprocity, the audacity of mutuality. It is the revolution of the spirit made visible through everyday tenderness: a word spoken with care, a silence held without judgment, a small act that restores dignity where humiliation once reigned.

Here Jung's warning returns: the subtlest corruption is always self-betrayal—the Judas within, the quiet turning away from what we know to be true. And Sayadaw U Pandita's voice echoes beside him: it is not enough to know the *Dhamma*; we must become it—breathe it until it breathes us, live it until it becomes our oxygen.

This, then, is the art of non-self-betrayal—not posture or performance, but the naked intimacy of authenticity lived without disguise. A life steeped in *mettā*—loving-kindness extended not only to the virtuous self we wish to be, but also to the absurd, frightened, beautiful creatures we are. Humor, too, belongs to this path, for laughter disarms the tyrant within and keeps the revolution from turning into religion. As Wilde might have said, most people die of their personas long before their bodies are informed.

But the deeper truth remains: without self-betrayal there can be no tyranny; without self-betrayal, no collusion with power. Where self-betrayal ends, the revolution of the spirit begins—a quiet uprising that renders politics porous to grace, transforming governance into prayer, and allowing the world, once again, to breathe.

Section VIII:
The Radiance of Resistance

❋

Aung San Suu Kyi, the Divine Feminine, and the Revolution of the Spirit

Five years later, in 1995, when I first met Aung San Suu Kyi, it was through the good offices of my dear friend and mentor, Saya U Tin Oo. After co-founding the National League for Democracy in 1989—a party rooted in nonviolence, dialogue, and reconciliation with the regime—he was imprisoned yet again by Burma's military strongman, Ne Win. Caged in solitary confinement for another six years, he endured what would have broken most men. When he was finally released, he led me to Aung San Suu Kyi's family home on University Avenue in Rangoon.

By then, *Daw Suu*—as she was called across Burma—had only just emerged from six years of house arrest. During that time, in 1991, she was awarded the Nobel Peace Prize for leading her country's unwavering commitment to nonviolent revolution.

My own return to Burma in 1995 came following an invitation from a French publisher, who asked me to attempt re-entry and invite Aung San Suu Kyi to share her story of nonviolent struggle with the world. She agreed—on one non-negotiable condition: that her two closest colleagues and mentors, U Tin Oo and U Kyi Maung (who had also endured long years in solitary confinement), be included too.

Armed soldiers and police were stationed at her gate, a permanent theater of intimidation. Rifles at the ready, eyes unblinking, notebooks in hand. Every arrival noted, every departure scrutinized. And so, I sat with her in that modest family home, beneath the shadow of constant surveillance. With candor, she said to me: *"They want to know how I think."*

The weight of her words was unmistakable. These men were not there to guard her—they were there to contain her radiance, to dissect her mind as if it were Burma's most dangerous weapon. And yet, she carried it all with a composure that quietly unraveled the very purpose of their presence.

Freedom of Spirit

From the first moment, she was captivating. Poised. Eloquent. Uncompromising. Ethical. Witty. Piercingly intelligent. And beyond all that, her presence seemed to radiate *Dhamma*—not as performance, not as posture, but as an effortless *fragrance* of being.

Then, with a sudden sparkle in her eyes, she tilted her head and quipped, *"So let's not disappoint them, then."* And she laughed. Not nervously. Not to deflect. But a laugh that pierced the tension, mocked fear itself, and reclaimed the air as hers. In that laugh, she revealed her secret weapon: *freedom of spirit.* Even under siege, she breathed as one already free.

She carried herself with grace, a stillness at the center of the storm. A woman who chose love over hatred, again and again, when hatred would have been the easier path. Who chose kindness over vilification, not as strategy but as breath itself. Nonviolence wasn't her philosophy—it was her atmosphere. She inhaled it. She exhaled it. She embodied it.

And she proved it in the most dangerous way imaginable: by looking directly into the eyes of her captors—men armed to the teeth, men who had stripped her of freedom, of family, of years of her life—and saying, with quiet conviction: *"I do not hate you. I will not vilify you. I seek harmony with you—the peaceful coexistence of all our people."*

It wasn't naïveté. It wasn't submission. It was the fiercest defiance— the radical refusal to dehumanize. Because to love where hatred is demanded, to humanize where cruelty is enforced—*that is rebellion in its purest form. A politics of the heart.*

The Voice of Hope

Inside her home on University Avenue, Aung San Suu Kyi invited me into her world. For six months, in secret, we spoke. We recorded our conversations. She herself titled the book: *The Voice of Hope.*

She told me, looking directly into my eyes: "Alan, the revolution must not demonize—not even the dictator. Each man has in him the potential to realize the truth through his own will and endeavor—and to help others realize it. Human life therefore is infinitely precious."

And she went further: "Despotic governments do not recognize the precious human component of the state. They see citizens as a faceless, mindless, helpless mass to be manipulated at will. It is as though people were incidental to a nation rather than its very life-blood.

Patriotism, which should be the vital love and care of a people for their land, is debased into a smokescreen of hysteria to hide the injustices of authoritarian rulers who define the state only in terms of their own interests."

These weren't abstractions for her—they were *spiritual imperatives*. Daw Suu spoke not only of democracy and nonviolence, but of conscience as the deepest form of power. She spoke of the spiritual core of politics—that democracy without dignity is hollow, that freedom without compassion corrodes into cruelty, and that power without responsibility rots into tyranny.

The transcripts of our conversations—smuggled out of Burma— emerged as *The Voice of Hope: Conversations with Aung San Suu Kyi, Burma's Nobel Peace Laureate*. Translated into numerous languages, the book offered profound insight into totalitarianism, dictatorship, mind control, freedom, *the Dhamma of politics*, and nonviolent revolution. One reviewer for *The Observer* in London wrote: *"Whatever Burma's fate, a possible future for politics itself is illuminated by these conversations."*

Burma's Chorus of Conscience

And it was not just her. This ethos—the refusal to vilify, the commitment to conscience, the practice of nonviolence—was the *living marrow* of her entire political movement. Her teachers. Her mentors. Her colleagues. Men and women of rare moral and spiritual leadership, whose depth of humanity was stunning.

I was blessed to meet almost all of them—the ones still alive, not executed, tortured to death, or disappeared. Over an eight-year period, after being blacklisted from Burma for seventeen years and then finally unbanned, I interviewed more than two hundred former political prisoners—her allies, comrades, and friends—courageous souls who had endured years, sometimes decades, behind bars. Out of those conversations emerged *Burma's Voices of Freedom*—a four-volume chronicle of truth and resilience, co-created with my long-time collaborator Fergus Harlow.

And their words still ring:

"They could torture my body, but they could not make me hate."

"To forgive was to remain human, to not become like them."

"Even in the darkest cell, I still had my conscience, and that was my freedom."

This is the wisdom of revolutionary Burma. A collective testimony of those who chose love over hate, conscience over collusion, dignity over despair.

The Legacy of U Kyi Maung

I had also spent the previous six months with this man—his family, his friends, his colleagues—almost every day. And on my final day in Burma, in 1996, I sat with U Kyi Maung: Aung San Suu Kyi's colleague, her mentor, and one of the great statesmen of Burma's nonviolent revolution. He was eighty years old. Eleven of those years had been spent in solitary confinement.

Outside his compound, soldiers loyal to the dictatorship lingered with rifles ready. At any moment, I feared they would drag him away again. And so, I asked him, quietly, "Sir, if you are re-arrested, what words would you want to leave for the next generation of freedom fighters?"

He paused, closed his eyes for a moment, and then spoke, as if weighing each syllable against the scales of history: "Two things matter most: education and a deep sense of history. Knowledge is essential— not only of Burma, but of the world. And history—because to grasp it is to grasp our interrelatedness, the causes and consequences of thought and action. Every person plays a part. The gift of life is to play that part with responsibility."

And then he added something even more radical: "What I guard most is awareness. Just to be present. Awake. In prison I trained my mind to notice everything: the flicker of shadow on a wall, the sound of my own breath. That awareness was my freedom. I fear only one thing— that I might lose it. Because without awareness, we betray ourselves. And without awareness, civilization itself collapses."

That was his revolution: not anger, not revenge, but *awareness*. The refusal of self-betrayal.

And here his wisdom touched the same truth others have named in different tongues: that we exist only through one another. *Ubuntu—I am because you are*. In Burma, U Kyi Maung lived it. His practice of awareness was not a private escape from suffering, but a radical act of belonging. He showed me that awareness is never solitary—it is relational. To betray yourself is to betray the whole. To honor your conscience is to nourish the very fabric that binds us together.

That afternoon, as he walked me to the door, he smiled and said with his characteristic warmth: *"Don't worry. When death comes, let it come. What I fear most is not death, but becoming weak—lying in bed all day reading about the fall of yet another totalitarian regime."*

I had a tear in my eye as I left, not knowing it would be the last time I saw him. A number of years later, I was told he had passed—struck mid-sentence at dinner, while laughing. *Laughter was the final punctuation of his life.*

And so, his final gift to me endures: the reminder that Burma's struggle for freedom was never *somewhere else*. It has always been *here*—in the marrow of our interdependence, in the radical practice of awareness, in the quiet refusal of self-betrayal. His revolution was not bound by geography or time. It was—and remains—an invitation to each of us: to live awake, to live in conscience, to live as if the whole world depends on it. To embody, in our own imperfect ways, *a politics of the heart.*

Vilification in the West

And yet, to many in the West, Aung San Suu Kyi was publicly crucified in effigy for her so-called "silence," her alleged unwillingness to speak up for the Rohingya. Instead of reckoning with the junta's direct culpability, she was repeatedly criticized by *The New York Times, BBC,* and other outlets—fed into the same algorithm of distortion that devours inconvenient truths. Painted as a pariah, dismissed with words that bore no resemblance to the living reality of who she was.

Though some have turned against her, portraying her as complicit in the Rohingya crisis, I ask you to look deeper. During our eight-year investigation, *Burma's Voices of Freedom,* we recorded repeated advocacy by Daw Suu for Rohingya citizenship, humanitarian protection, and independent inquiries into military abuses—even as her civilian government operated under a constitution that gave the military full control over security.

What happened to the Rohingya was an atrocity. But to conflate her with the crime is to join the perpetrators in their deception. The junta weaponized tragedy to erase its own culpability—and much of the Western media, seduced by the moral thrill of outrage, became its unwitting accomplice.

I happened to be in Burma during much of this crisis. I heard directly from the very leaders and colleagues who were navigating this impossible terrain. I was there when her trusted ally and lawyer, Ko Ni—a Muslim from Rakhine State—worked with Daw Suu to challenge the illegal, military-drafted 2008 constitution. His aim was to dismantle the dictatorship's grip on power through law. For that courage, he was assassinated in broad daylight, gunned down at Yangon International Airport while holding his grandson. That single act said more about the junta's fear than any headline ever could.

The result was not truth but projection. *As Jung warned, those who refuse to face their own shadows will always crucify someone else's light.* Media elites deflected attention from the generals' crimes and heaped it on the one leader they most feared.

The consequences are not abstract. They are happening now. Over twenty-two thousand democratic leaders and activists languish in prison—silenced, tortured, starved, disappeared. More than one hundred thousand homes have been bombed or burned. Nearly ten thousand killed. Twenty million people require urgent humanitarian aid. Three and a half million have been displaced. Through it all, the very dictatorship that engineered this catastrophe continues to weaponize the distortions once parroted in Western headlines.

Let us be clear: this was not criticism—it was a global act of scapegoating, a misogynistic pageant disguised as moral concern. A witch-hunt against a woman who refused to conform to the script of pliant saint or compliant victim. For daring to be uncontrollable, she was branded arrogant, narcissistic, authoritarian. The establishment that profits from both war and self-righteousness mocked the one woman who practiced reconciliation as a state of mind.

Forgive my bluntness, but she is not just a symbol. She is my friend, my comrade in the art of fearless compassion.

Why This Book Exists

And it is their voices—alongside Daw Suu's—that my book *Conversation with a Dictator: A Challenge to the Authoritarian Assault* seeks *to* unsilence and enshrine. For today those same voices are once again behind bars—imprisoned, silenced, threatened with erasure.

But they are not gone. They endure in the marrow of resistance—in the courage to forgive without erasing memory, in the defiance to love without vilifying, in the stamina to hope without guarantees.

That is why *Conversation with a Dictator* exists: to carry their spirit forward. To remind the world that even in chains, even under torture, even in the darkest solitude—the revolution of the spirit does not die; it breathes, learns, and evolves.

And I remember Saya U Tin Oo—my Burmese general friend and mentor—who became a Buddhist monk and later returned as a nonviolent political leader. He told me: *"The only way you survive solitary confinement is through love.* I imagined my wife. My children. My friends. Even the dictator who imprisoned me. I carried their faces, in lucid clarity, inside my heart. I smiled into their *Being*—dissolving fear, dissolving every residue of anger within me—and drew that love—*mettā*—back into the present, *until it filled me, until it lived within me."*

Then he looked at me, steady, unshaken, and added: *"Alan, you asked what it takes to survive the darkest times. It is human warmth. The memory of love, carried into the present, made real again."*

And I dare say, this was Jung's antidote to the ultimate corruption—the slow suicide of self-betrayal. Here in Myanmar, I came to know its counterforce: *The Revolution of the Spirit*—a refusal to collude with fear, a refusal to abandon one's own humanity, a refusal to betray what is most sacred, even in chains.

It was a glimpse into the extraordinary, embodied by some of the most courageous ethical *Dharma* warriors of modern times—perhaps of all time. *These were not metaphors; they were miracles in motion.* Proof that the spirit, when anchored in love, is unconquerable.

That is survival. That is *Dhamma*. That is revolution. And if history has any conscience left, it will remember that *the true power of Burma was never its generals—but its awakened hearts.*

Section IX:
The Parliament of the Heart

✳

The Discipline of Love in a World of Hatred

February 1, 2021: Before dawn, Senior General Min Aung Hlaing—third in an unbroken line of dictators after Ne Win and Than Shwe—extinguished the nation's most fragile hope for democracy.

Within weeks, thousands of lives were seized and silenced: the president, the cabinet, parliamentarians, activists. Doctors and mothers. Monks and teenagers. Teachers, artists, filmmakers. Entire families torn from their homes under cover of darkness. No one who dared to stand—or even whisper dissent—was spared.

And Aung San Suu Kyi—after fifteen years of detentions—was again silenced, entombed in a windowless cell: the regime's ultimate confession of fear before her still-unbroken moral authority, the enduring sovereign voice of her people.

Four years later, after the March 28, 2025 earthquake that devastated Sagaing, her legal team in Paris shared what appeared to be leaked—yet unconfirmed—reports: she was injured, her cell damaged. Those who understand Burma's language of cruelty knew what was being implied. Was it Min Aung Hlaing's way of telling the world, we did not kill her; the earth did—a dictator's alibi carved in catastrophe? As of today, we still do not know.

And for years, we have known only silence—no word, no letter, no visitor, no photograph, no proof of life. Only the hush of a prison where dignity itself is mocked, even as her son pleads that his mother is gravely ill with heart disease. The junta, in its cold arithmetic, dismisses it all as "fabrication," insisting she is perfectly healthy—even in a windowless, vermin-ridden cell.

The Revolution of Conscience

My *Dhamma* teacher in Burma—the late Venerable Sayadaw U Pandita—saw Burma broken by tyranny: Ne Win, Than Shwe, Min Aung Hlaing. He watched prisons fill, villages burn, families vanish. Yet he still believed in redemption. His warning was simple, and I carry it still: *do not let hatred become your collaborator. Do not mirror the cruelty you oppose.*

Because the proclivities of self-betrayal—anger, greed, prejudice, projection, ignorance, violence, domination—are not dictators' alone. They live in every human heart. As Sayadaw U Pandita reminded us: *"The duty of the Dhamma is to meet them face to face, to challenge them, to transform them, to overcome them—here, in this very life."*

Close your heart, and tyranny finds its most intimate accomplice: it colonizes your own psyche. Dictators endure not only by chains and guns, but by provoking the hatred that sustains their rule.

This is why the struggle for freedom is more than politics. It is an insurrection of the inner life—a revolution of conscience. The true parliament is not in palaces or prisons but within the human soul, where love and hate, denial and truth, collusion and courage cast their votes breath by breath. This, ultimately, is the *politics of the heart*—the unseen legislature of being, where freedom is not decreed but lived, where every act of awareness becomes a form of governance, and every pulse of compassion a law unto itself.

Aung San Suu Kyi embodied this revolution. After fifteen years of detention, and now locked in solitary confinement, she still insisted on reconciliation—even toward those who tortured and murdered her people. That was not political strategy. *That was Dhamma alive.* That was the revolution of conscience—embodied, unbowed, unbroken.

The Casualness of Evil and the Necessity of Imagination

Let me say plainly what this book is. *Conversation with a Dictator* is a staging ground where conscience interrogates power. It is not a refuge, not a performance of outrage, and certainly not therapy for despair. It is an encounter—constructed with words and images—designed to test a single proposition: can a human being, armored in ideology and insulated by fear, still feel the tug of conscience?

So, I invite him—in imagination—into the most flattering room he knows: his own palace. Not humiliate him, not to appease him, but to ask what he will not ask himself.

Could shame arise without collapse into self-pity? Could the dignity of his people become visible to him as his own dignity? Could a sentence as small and seismic as "I was wrong" cross his lips?

You hear the risk already: naïveté on one side, cynicism on the other. I refuse both. Moral imagination is neither a lullaby nor a slogan; it is a discipline—a willingness to picture a future in which repair is possible, while refusing to falsify the past that requires it.

I worked in deliberate solitude. A chosen exile of attention. Days dissolved into nights reading testimony; listening to survivors; diagramming the grammar of fear; studying how bureaucracies launder cruelty into procedure; how doctrine licenses indifference; how a lie, repeated in ritual cadence, becomes a room one can live in. I was not compiling a chronicle; I was tracing a physiology of harm: how dread congeals into policy, how the hunger for control corrodes judgment, how the self kills off inconvenient truths to preserve its fictions.

That inquiry demanded I look inward with the same severity. The tyrant in miniature—mine and yours—is not a metaphor. He appears in the reflex to dominate a conversation, in the pleasure of vilification, in the quiet arithmetic that weighs other people's pain against our convenience. If the book did not expose him in me, it would forfeit the authority to expose him in anyone.

The Anatomy of Evil

Evil does not begin with violence. It begins with fear. Fear manufactures myth. A wound is renamed "order." A purge is renamed "security." Fear cloaks itself in necessity and, in doing so, forges the first lie.

Myth then hides machinery. The banality of budgets, chains of command, procurement schedules, reports stacked in binders. Atrocity is not born in chaos; it is budgeted. It is designed, calculated, and managed by clerks and officers who assure themselves they are only "doing their jobs."

Machinery demands euphemism. Massacre becomes "stabilization." Murder becomes "neutralization." Bombing villages becomes "kinetic activity." Starvation becomes "population management." Euphemism numbs the tongue, corrodes perception, severs words from reality.

And when words are corrupted, reality itself is corroded. Language no longer points to truth; it tranquilizes us against it. Once atrocity has been rebranded, suffering can be commodified—packaged, outsourced, consumed.

This corrosion breeds spectatorship. Suffering no longer breaks our hearts; it becomes content. A dead child is a headline. A burned village is a thirty-second clip. Atrocity becomes something to scroll past.

And spectatorship recruits complicity. We are no longer asked to believe, or even to agree. We are only asked to look away. To look away again. To keep looking away.

This is what I mean by the casualness of evil: not theatrical cruelty, but the daily normalization of it—the routine memo, the algorithmic nudge, the headline engineered to evade the word that would force a reckoning. "Enhanced interrogation." "Precision strike." "Human terrain." "Development zone." A lexicon not to reveal but to conceal; to persuade us that what is happening is anything but what it is.

The Counter-Lexicon

A counter-lexicon is needed—one that restores meaning without surrendering to the *amphetamine* of fury. Here the *Dharma* is not an ornament; it is the method. *Yoniso manasikāra*—wise attention—asks us to look closely enough to see causes and conditions, to notice how hatred recruits us into its circuitry, to interrupt the momentum of harm before it hardens into fate. *Satipaṭṭhāna*—mindfulness joined with discernment—refuses both denial and despair. And *mettā* and *karuṇā*—loving-kindness and compassion—do not license impunity; they prevent us from becoming functionaries of the very cruelty we oppose.

Shame and guilt deserve a word here. Shame without a path to repair collapses into hiding. Guilt, honestly faced, can ripen into responsibility. The imagined dialogue in this book is engineered to pry open that hinge—not to stage a ritual of degradation, but to make remorse plausible without falsifying the damage that demands justice. *Reconciliation is not an escape from accountability; it is accountability with a future.*

Why Words and Images Matter

Why the images? Because dictatorship is not only a doctrine; it is an atmosphere—a pressure on the chest, a distortion of time, a calculated silence. Black-and-white is not an aesthetic flourish; it is the *moral chiaroscuro* of the work. Light and shadow make arguments no paragraph can. Negative space testifies to absence. The face of a child dissolving into ash can speak more than a thousand pages. The silence of a cell can embody complicity more than any speech. And Aung San Suu Kyi herself—erased in reality, no word, no photograph, no proof of life—is resurrected here in image: lotus, shadow, sovereign. She is an absence that refuses erasure.

The Template Travels

And why insist this book speaks beyond Burma? Because the template travels. It rides on surveillance and spectacle, on the commerce of attention, on the habit—left, right, secular, religious—of bending language until the unsayable can be said without consequence. The geographies differ; the mechanisms rhyme: law transmuted into *lawfare*, emergencies made permanent, propaganda braided with entertainment, the economy of clicks disciplining what can be seen. From Myanmar to Ukraine, Beijing to Tehran, Washington to Silicon Valley—the architecture is shared: suppress dissent, distort truth, weaponize fear.

I am not interested in scolding the world. I am interested in recruiting it. We need artists and engineers, monks and mothers, students and strategists—people willing to practice an ethics of attention and an aesthetics of truth. To name what is happening cleanly. To refuse the invitation to hate. To cultivate the fortitude required for real change. To act now with the clarity that prevents one more child from vanishing into the machinery of a policy whose name was designed to keep us from noticing. This is, in essence, the *politics of the heart*—the courage to transform awareness into action, and compassion into power.

The Summons to Repair

So, if you ask what this book is for, I will answer this: It is a device for *slowing the lie* until you can hear it fracture. It is a room where a man armored in delusion can be asked a question he cannot escape. It is a lens for seeing how institutions turn fear into routine. It is a reminder that attention is a moral act. It is a summons to repair.

I will not pretend that a dialogue on paper can disarm a drone. But sentences can dissolve inevitabilities; images can puncture the spell that makes cruelty feel like weather. Culture is not an accessory to politics; it is the factory where politics is forged.

So yes, this work is literature. But literature as scalpel, compass, alarm. A mirror and a hammer. A prayer and a witness. Against the casualness of evil, cleverness will never suffice. *Only a revolution of conscience*—how we see, speak, and stand with one another—can meet it.

That revolution begins—in this book, in this room, in this breath—with the refusal to look away, and the courage to name what things are. And if we are brave, it does not end there; it matures into the only politics worthy of love. *A politics of the heart.*

Or, as Wilde might have said today: *if your conscience needs costume jewelry, it's auditioning for a part you don't want to play.*

Section X:
The Pathology of Normalized Atrocity

❋

The Dream-Life Beside the Death Camp

Think of *The Zone of Interest*—the harrowing 2023 film written and directed by Jonathan Glazer, loosely based on the novel by Martin Amis. It tells the story of Rudolf Höss, the Auschwitz commandant, and his wife Hedwig, who construct a life of contrived normalcy in a villa pressed against the wall of industrialized extermination. She arranges flowers while the wind carries the smoke of burning bodies. He sips tea on the terrace while, just beyond the hedge, prisoners collapse under whips and starvation. Their children splash in the pool while other children—unseen but not unheard—are herded into chambers of death.

The genius—and the terror—of the film is its *austere restraint*. Evil is not staged as spectacle but revealed as domestic routine. The camera lingers not on gas chambers, but on laundry lines, breakfast tables, manicured gardens—ordinary gestures performed beside extraordinary cruelty. The soundscape does the rest: muffled screams, gunshots, furnaces. It reveals that atrocity endures not only through the machinery of killers, but through the delusion of pretense—the numbing that blinds those who refuse to see.

And that is why it unsettles: because it is not only about them—the Nazis. It is about us. It is about the human capacity to compartmentalize reality, to turn the unbearable into background noise, to cultivate beauty on one side of the hedge while ashes fall on the other. It is about the *willful blindness* that downgrades us into treating others as expendable matter—lives dismissed as collateral, suffering renamed as necessity. It is about the instinct to build walls high enough to conceal truth, even as it seeps through the cracks.

This is the pathology of evil at its most insidious: not only its violence, but its *normalization*. Atrocity assimilated into domestic ritual. Genocide camouflaged by birthday parties and Sunday tea. Language conscripted into the lie—manufacturing a dream of security while colluding in annihilation. It exposes the ultimate self-betrayal: *a psyche split in two, sustained by the refusal to see, anesthetized by pretense, purchased at the price of another's breath."*

Gaza, Ukraine, Burma, America

That pathology did not end at Auschwitz. It is alive today, metastasized across the globe, dressed in new uniforms and digitized for mass consumption.

We see it in Gaza: children starving to death while drones circle overhead, reducing entire neighborhoods to rubble. A mother tearing at concrete with bloodied hands in search of her daughter's arm. Families erased in an instant—names, faces, futures eradicated from memory as if they never existed. The images flicker across our screens, and we scroll. *This is how numbness becomes normalized.*

And here I must invoke the unflinching witness of Shoug Mukhaimar, a young Palestinian writer and student of English literature at Al-Aqsa University, who dares to write what few can bear to say: "We no longer have the strength to pray. Please, don't ask us to have hope anymore."

She testifies that the famine is not the most terrible thing in Gaza—the greater atrocity is the systematic killing of hope. "We are bombed, starved, displaced—and then the news finishes us off. This is deliberate policy. Hope raised, then shattered. A machinery of torment designed to break us, to strip us of the basic human right to dream of tomorrow."

She describes children who "no longer cry when their brothers are bombed to pieces, who no longer ask for food even as their bellies burn, who no longer beg for help because they know none will come."

What does it mean when a child no longer hopes? It means evil has become *normalized.* It means innocence itself has been desecrated, extinguished, turned into silence.

And Shoug asks the question that should haunt every conscience: *"How can an entire planet watch two million people starved, bombed, stripped of dignity—and still do nothing?"*

This silence is complicity. It crushes as much as hunger does. It whispers that these lives are expendable, that their vanishing is acceptable. History will condemn not only those who committed these crimes, but also those who stood by and watched.

And so, I ask you—what could possibly stop this? Not another U.N. resolution. Not another diplomatic pause. And not only in Gaza. The pathology metastasizes across Ukraine, Russia, Myanmar (Burma),

Sudan, and here in America, too—in the algorithms of indifference, the economies of distraction, the politics of dehumanization. And it is not new. It has stalked history like a shadow.

And yes, as of today—October 13, 2025—a Middle East peace accord *born* of genocide is reportedly underway, with Israeli hostages and Palestinian prisoners and detainees being returned; yet Gaza resembles Dresden in 1945: an expanse of rubble and twisted carcasses of buildings, the air is heavy with the smell of death, and trauma etched into every molecule of those who remain alive.

What have we learned?

A Century of Atrocity

Mao's China: tens of millions starved.

Stalin's USSR: millions gulagged, executed, disappeared.

Indigenous genocide: Americas, Canada, Australia—nations erased by massacre, smallpox, starvation.

Cambodia's killing fields: two million exterminated.

The Holocaust: six million Jews—and millions more—systematically murdered.

The Congo Free State: ten million whipped, starved, worked to death.

Rwanda: in one hundred days, 800,000 butchered.

Armenia: 1.5 million annihilated.

Bosnia, Srebrenica: 8,000 massacred in a single week.

Hiroshima and Nagasaki: 200,000 vaporized.

On and on it goes, the record of empire and nation, of ideology and religion, soaked in blood. *The pathology of patriarchy*, the cult of dominance, embedded like shrapnel in the DNA of consciousness.

The Commerce of Looking Away

We see it in Ukraine: apartment blocks collapsing under Russian missiles, fathers carrying the limp bodies of their children down smoke-filled stairwells, mass graves carved into frozen earth, black bags stacked in rows like broken punctuation marks in history. And yet, in distant capitals, politicians gather at banquets to debate sanctions, insulated from the smell of charred flesh. *Normalized*—because distance excuses feeling.

We see it in Burma: villages torched by soldiers, infants burned alive, students executed in the street, women raped in front of their families; entire populations driven into the jungle where malaria and starvation finish what bullets began, while in *Naypyidaw*, the generals raise their glasses beneath chandeliers—drunk on blood, drunk on power—and call it order. *Normalized.*

We see it in America too: classrooms turned into killing fields, backpacks soaked through, small bodies carried past microphones where officials mouth "thoughts and prayers" and then cash the checks that help keep the carnage solvent. Children sacrificed to commerce. And after the cameras pack up, the committee hearings and fundraisers resume on schedule. *Normalized —because impunity rehearsed becomes impunity repeated.*

Name the pattern clearly: atrocity, euphemism, amnesia, repeat. A massacre becomes "stabilization," a bribe becomes "speech," a curfew becomes "security," and we acclimate by inches until the unacceptable feels inevitable. This is how democracies rot from the inside: not by a single coup, but by the slow manipulation of language and the profitable boredom of business as usual.

Only an uprising of conscience—a *politics of the heart,* fierce enough to rip through the narcotic of normalization—can break this cycle. Courageous citizens who refuse derision as policy, refuse fear as governance, refuse to trade children's lives for quarterly returns; artists, monks, nurses, coders, poets, teachers, farmers, veterans, and students willing to practice a daily discipline of truth-telling that denies cruelty the camouflage of custom.

Because when two million people are left to disappear in plain sight, it is not only Gaza that dies—it is civilization's claim to itself. So, say it without makeup or marketing: is this "peace accord" a path to repair, or another euphemism that keeps the cash flowing to industrialized slaughter?

The Civilization of Numbness

This is the dream-life beside the death camp. This is the garden party beside the gas chamber. This is our civilization: a planet that has made peace with atrocity. A world anesthetized by spectacle, distraction, euphemism. A culture that scrolls past screams.

Why *Conversation with a Dictator* Exists

And that is why I wrote *Conversation with a Dictator*: to resist the narcotic of normalization. To make silence impossible. To tear away the veil of neutrality and expose what we already know but dare not face.

Because history is not a museum piece—it is alive, happening now, in Ukraine, in Sudan and Myanmar, in prisons, in refugee camps, in boardrooms of quiet compliance and newsfeeds of programmed consent.

This book exists to say: atrocity does not arrive fully grown. It germinates in self-betrayal, in the daily collusions of silence, in the small concessions we make to fear and convenience.

It exists to remind us that dictatorship is not only a Burmese story, or a Nazi story—*it is the architecture of power wherever conscience is suppressed.* It thrives when people stop asking questions, when propaganda is swallowed as truth, when neighbors stop seeing each other as human.

It exists to rehumanize what tyranny dehumanizes. To bear witness where propaganda erases. To say the unsayable. To remember the disappeared. *To dignify the broken.*

And finally, this book exists because we are not powerless. The revolution of the spirit is not history's footnote—it is its *lifeline*.

That is also why *Conversation with a Dictator* exists: to remind us that freedom is not a flag or a ballot box. Freedom is a refusal—the refusal to violently vilify, the refusal to collude with fear, the refusal to betray oneself, the refusal to look away.

Aung San Suu Kyi once told me: *"Alan, empathy and compassion make good people quiver. That is the revolution."*

"To mindfully and self-responsibly feel is dangerous," she said, *"for it unsettles the order of indifference and hatred. Empathy disrupts obedience. Compassion corrodes authoritarian control."*

The true turning of the mind is not hatred amplified, but conscience *awakened*— the courage to tremble before suffering rather than turn away, to let discomfort break us open rather than harden into violence or dissolve into numbness.

The Pathology Within

This book is not merely about Burma, nor about one dictator. It is about the normalization of violence as the default condition of the modern world. It is about the loss of wonder—the slow erasure of reverence beneath the noise of comfort. Where violence and atrocity are rebranded as security, oppression is rationalized as policy, and denial elevated to the status of governance.

The pathology is not confined to palaces, parliaments, or barracks. It nests in the psyche. It coils in denial. It hides in self-deception. It thrives in the silence of complicity.

That is why this work speaks not only to generals and presidents, but to artists, monks, mothers, students, engineers, teachers, poets, imams, rabbis, and priests. *For authoritarianism is not only a political condition—it is a spiritual one.* It is not merely imposed upon us; it seduces us. It recruits us. It feeds on our fear, our fatigue, our temptation to vilify, our craving to look away.

And so, the challenge is not only external but internal: can we restrain the hatred that mirrors the tyrant's own? Can we speak truth without weaponizing it into vengeance? Can we resist cruelty without reproducing its logic?

To the Architects of Silence

I direct these words not only to the visible architects of violence and war—even those who disguise destruction as "peacebuilding"—but to the world's policymakers and power brokers, the stewards of empires and economies, the ones who decide which lives are expendable for "security" or "progress."

And further still: to the corporate mandarins and technocrats who profit from annihilation—the arms merchants, the data lords, the financiers of precision death—who launder slaughter in the language of "innovation" and "defense." To the investors and shareholders who monetize the machinery of misery, and to the bureaucrats of silence who approve each contract as though they were signing a weather report.

But let us be clear: this indictment reaches far beyond presidents, ministers, and CEOs. It extends to every official, pundit, and policymaker who profits from silence—or from the weaponization of words. To every artist or intellectual who chooses self-censorship over conscience. And to every citizen tempted not only to mistake neutrality for innocence, but to embrace the seduction of contempt—to reduce human beings to abstractions, to feed the algorithm of division while tyranny fattens on the spectacle.

The pathology of violence endures because we allow it to endure. We must name it, feel it, and end it. For violence today is not only the bullet, the bomb, or the cage—it is also the corruption of language: words twisted into weapons, sharpened to incite polarization, to radicalize neighbor against neighbor, to make cruelty feel righteous.

It is the politics of contempt masquerading as debate, the steady drip of demonization that corrodes trust and community. It is rhetorical poison that turns citizens into combatants, priming them to desecrate, violate, even kill in the name of their indoctrinated illusions of "rightness."

We must lay it down—the weapon of hate, the weapon of prejudice, the weapon of fear disguised as patriotism. Every ideology of domination that fattens itself on ignorance and greed. We must also lay down the narratives that pit tribe against tribe, the propaganda that whispers violence into the mind and calls it virtue.

To step out of the machinery of retribution is an act of conscience. For war is not liberation—it is desecration. Violence is Stone Age barbarism dressed up as strategy. *And murder—whether justified by nation, profit, or God—remains murder.*

Scream to Stop the Killing

So, feel the weight of the bodies decomposing on the streets of Gaza, Kyiv, Aleppo, Mandalay. Feel the mothers clawing through rubble with bare hands. Feel the children gasping their last breath beneath collapsed concrete. And know: your missiles, your drones, your bureaucracies and algorithms of death wrote those names in blood. You dare call it freedom. You dare call it democracy. You dare call it God.

And do not think this violence belongs only to "somewhere else."

It lives here—in our own regions, states, cities, towns, and homes. It erupts in our schools, where children rehearse survival instead of songs. It stalks our colleges, where ideas are drowned out by threats and rage. It enters our churches, synagogues, mosques, and temples, where sanctuaries of faith are desecrated with blood. It seeps into our politics, where leaders trade in vilification, where words become weapons, and where demonization radicalizes neighbors into enemies. From the supermarket aisle to the ballot box, from social media feeds to the halls of Congress, the machinery of violence has come home.

Stop. Stop in the name of humanity. Stop in the name of love. Stop before there is nothing left to stop.

This is the revolution we need: not the scream of hate, but the restraint born of love. Not the silence of fear, but the courage of conscience—even when it must scream. Yes, scream—but scream to stop the killing. Scream until tyrants tremble, until children rise, until tenderness returns to power. Scream until compassion becomes our common tongue, and the heart reclaims its rightful place as the seat of all politics—*a politics of the heart.*

The Necessary Evil?

There will be those among you—maybe even in this room—who think: Yes, killing is tragic. Yes, war is obscene. But sometimes, it is necessary. The "necessary evil," they call it. The lesser of two horrors.

But let us be unsparingly honest: that phrase is the heroin of history—potent, seductive, and terminal. It is how slavery was justified. It is how colonialism was defended. It is how Hiroshima was rationalized. Always: "necessary." Always: "inevitable." Always: "for the greater good."

This is how the normalization of insanity works. We convince ourselves that cruelty is reason, that domination is duty, that the destruction of life is the preservation of order. We wrap the abyss in logic, baptize the madness in language, sanctify the corpse and call it progress. We call it patriotism, deterrence, divine will. And we forget the blood trails of history—Lincoln, Gandhi, King, Kennedy, Biko, Benazir—all struck down by the same anesthetized righteousness, the same sanctified madness.

The Cult of Domination

And what is at the root of this reflex? It is *the* unexamined *patriarchal* imagination—the ancient cult of domination in which power is equated with control, manhood is measured by conquest, and leadership is confused with the capacity to command obedience at the barrel of a gun.

This is not merely a cultural habit but a civilizational pathology: *a worldview that sanctifies hierarchy, normalizes subjugation, and exalts violence as the ultimate arbiter of truth.* It is a sickness so deeply woven into our myths, our institutions, and our collective unconscious that we scarcely recognize it. And yet, left unchallenged, it devours everything—eros, community, democracy, even the possibility of a shared humanity.

The Revolution of Conscience

Leadership is not conquest. Leadership is conscience in action. Leadership is restraint when rage would be easier, dialogue when violence would be faster, listening when shouting would be louder. *True leadership is the refusal to mirror the insanity of "necessary evil."*

And what must we learn in this moment of unraveling? *The essential wisdom of nonviolence*—not as passive submission, but as the fine art of managing difference and disagreement without collapsing into destruction. The bold and courageous skill of *anger alchemy*, so that anger can be transmuted into clarity rather than carnage. The elevation of evolving freedom and democracy, rather than the primitive urge to "kill off" your so-called demonic enemy—whether you label them fascist, communist, extremist, or heretic. For language itself has become a weapon, distorted to fit narratives that justify annihilation.

Because someone—somewhere—must stop this spiral. Someone must stand and say: *enough.* Enough of the mythology of inevitability. *Enough of the patriarchal theater of war.* Enough of calling death a strategy.

And this is why dialogue matters. Why discussion matters. Why the discipline of restraint matters. Because every bomb dropped is a failure of imagination. Every massacre is a confession that we could not bear to speak, to listen, to stay in the room until the madness cracked.

The revolution of conscience does not begin when we win a war. It begins when we dare to turn toward one another instead of away. It begins when leadership is no longer measured by domination, but by the audacity to imagine that peace is not naïve—that *peace is the most radical, the most courageous, the most necessary act of all.*

Beyond War, Toward Humanity

The real struggle before us is not between nations or parties, but between *annihilation and imagination,* between the death-drive of domination and the life-force of conscience. To choose peace is not weakness; it is the deepest form of strength. To choose dialogue is not delay; it is the only path that averts catastrophe. To choose love in the face of hatred is not naïve; it is the most disciplined act of defiance.

The future will not be secured by those who perfect the machinery of killing, but by those who dismantle it. It will belong to those bold enough to reject the mythology of "necessary evil" and to build, instead, a civilization where freedom is not won by conquest but by compassion, and where democracy is not defended by war but by the *audacity of care.*

A Conversation with My Teacher

I asked such questions many times of my beloved *Dhamma* teacher, the late Venerable Sayadaw U Pandita. How do you change the mind's set? How do you stop betraying yourself and causing harm—both to yourself and to others?

Let me recount one such conversation that has never left me. He turned me toward a teaching from the *Ambalaṭṭhika Rāhulovāda Sutta,* where the Buddha offered his young son, *Rāhula,* a lesson of timeless depth.

Rāhula was only seven, vibrant with innocence. The Buddha, seeing the seeds of leadership within him, chose not abstraction, not doctrine, but living images that the boy could carry for life.

He began with truthfulness. He poured a small measure of water into a cup. "Can you see how little there is?" he asked. *Rāhula* nodded. "So too," the Buddha said, "is the virtue of one who feels no shame in a deliberate lie." Then he poured the water out, overturned the cup, and showed it empty—each gesture a stark illustration of how deception empties the soul.

Next, he held up a mirror. "What is a mirror for?" he asked. "To reflect," *Rāhula* replied. The Buddha leaned in: "*So too, let your mind be a mirror.* Examine your thoughts, your words, your deeds—before, during, and after. See them with unsparing clarity. Own them with courage. Amend them with compassion."

And then came the threefold discipline of reflection:

Before acting: Will this harm myself or others?

During action: If harm begins to arise, pause and redirect.

After action: If harm was done, confess it, resolve, and begin again with mindfulness.

This was not a lesson in judgment, but in honesty, responsibility, and reverence for all life.

In Burmese monasteries, we are taught to live through the three doors of body, speech, and mind. Each door demands vigilance before we step through it. Wise reflection is not optional—it is the very cornerstone of ethical existence.

And here the spirit of *ubuntu*—I am because we are—is woven in. Every word, every deed, ripples across the shared waters of humanity:

A lie clouds the water.

A truth spoken polishes the mirror of trust.

An act of greed hardens the soil of connection.

An act of generosity renews it with hope.

Wise reflection, then, is not mere morality. *It is our shared salvation.*

In this light, *ubuntu* becomes a daily vow:

Before enacting laws, ask: Will this restore dignity or diminish it?

Before speaking, ask: Will this heal or harm?

Before acting, ask: Will this bridge division or deepen it?

And so, once more, allow me to offer the Buddha's *pāramīs*—the ten noble perfections—as living questions:

Dāna (Generosity): What can I give without seeking reward?

Sīla (Integrity): Can I align my actions with my deepest truth?

Nekkhamma (Renunciation): Can I let go of what binds me?

Paññā (Wisdom): Am I seeing clearly, or through the veil of ignorance?

Viriya (Energy): Can I persist without losing heart?

Khanti (Patience): Can I endure with tenderness intact?

Sacca (Truthfulness): Will I honor truth, even at great cost?

Adhiṭṭhāna (Determination): Will I remain steadfast through trials?

Mettā (Loving-kindness): Can I extend goodwill to all, without exception?

Upekkhā (Equanimity): Can I stand steady amid life's storms?

These are not abstractions. *They are beacons.* They are how conscience survives the dark.

And *ubuntu* is the mirror we polish with our lives.
It is not a phrase.
It is not a dream.
It is a choice.

A sacred vow whispered across generations: *We are bound to one another. Only together do we remain whole.*

Section XI:
The Therapy of Truth and the Politics of Imagination

❈

Dreamers and the Failed Experiment of Violence

Let's be frank—and I think most of us would agree—democracy, once envisioned as a covenant of conscience, is now convulsing beneath the weight of its own unspoken trauma.

You can feel it everywhere—in the air, in conversation, in headlines: the fatigue, the distrust, the sense that something essential has fractured. Authoritarian. Fascist. Dictator. Words once reserved for the darkest chapters of history now circulate through the mainstream media like background radiation. They mouth them like members of Stalin's, Mao's, or Hussein's inner circle—condemnation delivered with the intimacy of loyalty.

Our discourse has not merely broken down; it has been hollowed from within. Language has become theatre—no longer a bridge of meaning but a performance of allegiance—stripped of sincerity, stripped of intimacy, and often emptied of truth.

Across nations, and nowhere louder than America, failed revolutionaries and talk-show demagogues act out their rage as policy—a psychodrama of narcissism disguised as governance, where decency and persuasion have been replaced by performance and paywalls.

And forgive me if I sound melodramatic, but unless there is a collective intervention—a revolutionary therapy of truth and conscience fierce enough to pierce our self-deception, our hubris, our *cultivated insanity*—there soon may be no world left to save.

The Anxiety of the Everyday

Many people I speak with confess the same thing: that they live each day on edge, uncertain, quietly afraid of what lies ahead. Even the so-called awakened—the spiritual, the educated, the psychologically astute—admit to feeling the tremor of disorientation. Hope itself has become fragile, an act of faith rather than conviction.

Despite the "peace accords" and political promises, we remain besieged by violence in every dimension of life. And what we too easily call "violence" must be expanded—not only beyond the spectacle of destruction, but to include domination itself: the conquest impulse, the authoritarian reflex that metastasizes in the minds of elites, in boardrooms, senates, and algorithmic citadels where the currencies of profit, power, and control are brokered as virtues of governance—marketed as stability, as progress, even as care—for you, for us.

For that is where it germinates—not in the chaos of battlefields but in the quiet habits of mind that precede them. It begins softly—within the refined arrogance of those who mistake privilege for destiny. When provoked, this architecture of domination does not always erupt in spectacle; it seeps, expands, corrodes and consolidates—manifesting as the slow suffocation of imagination, the colonization of conscience—until, almost inevitably, it blooms into another war, another genocide, *another chapter of state sanctioned madness.*

The Faces Behind the Noise

And that is where we find ourselves now—staring into the faces behind the noise.

We know them already; we know their names: the architects of atrocity, the merchants of ruin, the profiteers of war, the clerics of division who baptize blood and discord as policy. They sit in palaces and parliaments, in boardrooms and tech labs, draped in the vestments of legitimacy, laundering devastation into rhetoric and polishing massacre until it sounds like governance.

Addicted to violence as order, they canonize war as peace's counterfeit—mistaking domination for stability, brutality for management, despair for design. They do not lead; they administer decay—supervising collapse with executive grace, converting agony into asset, ruin into revenue.

History is heavy with this delusion: empires carved their borders in blood and called it security; religions mounted crusades and named it salvation; nations stockpiled arsenals and spoke of deterrence as doctrine. Again and again, violence has been embalmed as necessity, as sacrifice, as the supposed price of civilization. Yet the "peace" it delivered was always brittle, spectral, temporary—an armistice with suffering rather than a covenant with life.

The Children Who Never Grew Up: Power Without Conscience

And if earlier I spoke of the Buddha teaching his child, let me speak now to the opposite: the boys who never became men—who govern as if conscience were expendable, who treat empathy like contraband.

For them, the therapy required is not for the wounded but for the armored; not for the vulnerable but for the invulnerable. Generals in pressed uniforms, politicians with rehearsed smiles, executives with polished brands—stage-managers of cruelty orchestrating death from safe distances, converting slaughter into data and damage-control.

And then there are the negotiators—the peace brokers in five-star resorts, sipping imported water beside infinity pools, drafting ceasefires that expire before the ink dries. They speak of compromise as if it were compassion, of strategy as if it were salvation—calculating how much blood a handshake can conceal.

These men—and some women as well—are not leaders but *ethical amputees*: souls cauterized against empathy, spiritually lobotomized, morally blind. Some may dismiss this as hyperbole, even hysteria—but what could be more deranged than mass murderers in suits, deleting children as if they were contaminants on a spreadsheet—an errand of hygiene, no more consequential than asking the maid to exterminate a few roaches in the basement.

Yet vulnerability is the seed of conscience, and where conscience is absent, power metastasizes into pathology—rebranding evil itself as policy. The "duty of the state," they call it—to stabilize the region, to protect the homeland from terrorists, infidels, heathens, the sick, the deranged, the monsters—our inhumans. It's the ancient theater of atrocity, rehearsed and refined: kill to preserve freedom, slaughter to defend faith, annihilate to save the world.

This pathology is older than history itself—perhaps older than time—its malice almost divine in its patience, almost beautiful in its precision: *the great cosmic bureaucracy of sanctioned annihilation.*

The Alibis of Atrocity: How Leaders Sanctify Violence

Let us be clear: no leader ever declares, "I lust for blood." They are more sophisticated, more practiced at disguise. They baptize slaughter in the borrowed language of freedom, peace, and democracy. They claim security while manufacturing fear. They justify carnage as sacrifice to necessity, as though the annihilation of innocents were an offering to progress.

These alibis are predictable, recycled across centuries:

- Freedom *recast as invasion.*
- Peace *rebranded as pacification.*
- Unity *twisted into ethnic cleansing.*
- Justice *mutated into revenge.*
- Civilization *masked as conquest.*

History is littered with euphemisms, each a mask for mass graves. The theater continues—atrocity staged with precision, while audiences, trained by fear, dulled by propaganda, mistake horror for necessity and, in cynicism, even rise to applaud.

This is collusion, not realism; pathology, not necessity. For no leader destroys life to govern it.

Yet, with party preservation as the priority, they initial orders with fountain pens or autopens engraved with family crests or national seals, as if patriotism itself sanctified the signature.

Maps of precision murder are spread before them like tablecloths, entire regions folded and refolded as napkins. A signature here, a line drawn there—whole communities erased under the banner of duty, betrayal recast as loyalty, atrocity disguised as anthem.

The men who authorize such erasures remain embalmed in ceremony, armored in protocol, insulated by ritual—shaking hands beneath chandeliers, posing before marble statues, their faces smooth with the certainty that consequence belongs only to others. They do not tremble. They do not weep. They sleep soundly—until history wakes them.

The Planetary Pestilence of Patriarchy

As noted earlier, we know their personal names—but names change. They come and go with each election, each coup, each corporate merger. What endures is the role—and the *mindset* behind it. *The psychology of domination is the real dynasty.* So let us speak of categories, not individuals, so there is no confusion.

I call them *the six planetary pestilences of patriarchy*: presidents, prime ministers, politicians, predators, pedophiles, and profiteers—figures who often cloak psychopathy in the garments of respectability, possessed by the pathology of power. Not all, but far too many—and this is where the vast machinery of killing begins.

They inherit the collective delirium of their predecessors—their ravages, their convulsions of insanity—and carry the legacy forward with bureaucratic precision. The killing machines get upgrades; the suits and uniforms stay the same. And when the moment calls for it, they love to flex their *alpha-murder muscle*—invoking the kill word, "deterrence," as if slaughter were a sacrament of peace, as if extinction were the cost of leadership. The ritual never ends—it just rebrands.

These *six archetypes of cruelty* are addicted to power, armored in entitlement, incapable—or unwilling—to feel the weight of the lives they extinguish. To call them "leaders" is not simply inaccurate—it is to desecrate the very meaning of leadership. Yet, for now, they are the stewards of our species, the ones holding the levers, however bloodstained. To refuse engagement is to abandon the field; to engage blindly is to become their echo. We must therefore learn new ways of working with them—innovative, creative, disarming—transforming confrontation into conscience, and strategy into moral intelligence. Because the end of tyranny will not come by its mirror, but by its re-imagination.

And before you react—let us be clear: history has shown exceptions. There have been leaders who resisted intoxication, who held power without being consumed by it, who tempered authority with conscience. But they are rare.

Their rarity only proves the rule: *true leadership is not the norm—it is the exception.*

We should treat it like a miracle and demand it like a standard.

Psychologies of Mass Murder: The Collapse of Conscience

We may be asking: what separates a serial killer in an alleyway from a man enthroned with an army at his command? Not morality—permission. The killer hides in shadows, fearing the law; the ruler orders massacres in daylight, violence paraded as policy. One kills in secret; the other choreographs slaughter as spectacle, draped in flags and anthems, rituals masquerading as sanctity while desecrating life itself.

Jung would say: they are possessed by archetypes—the Warrior, the Savior, the Patriarch—shadow-projections that demand an enemy to devour. *Freud would say:* they are vessels of the death drive, rationalized by a distorted superego until extermination feels like duty. *The Buddha would say:* they are blinded by *avijjā*, gripped by greed and hatred, clinging to delusions of permanence and control. And Camus would remind us: the real absurdity is not life itself but the willingness to destroy it in order to control it—*killing in the name of order is nothing less than a confession of failure to live in freedom.*

The Collapse of Empathy

And beneath it all, the collapse of empathy. Not its disappearance, but its distortion—the narrowing of feeling until it fits only within the borders of tribe, ideology, or flag. They cradle their own children while vaporizing another's, their compassion confined to a gated perimeter of belonging.

As mentioned earlier, this is not new. It is the ancient inheritance of domination—the same psychology of power that animates presidents and generals, profiteers and predators. What changes are the logos, the slogans, the weapons; what endures is the mindset: *a conscience programmed for selective mercy.*

They inherit not only the machinery of control, but the emotional architecture of empire—the learned incapacity to feel beyond one's own reflection. Each new generation upgrades the operating system of indifference, perfecting efficiency while erasing intimacy.

Empathy, when contracted, becomes propaganda. It blinds not through hatred but through hierarchy—the illusion that some lives are worth more than others. This is how atrocity sustains itself: not through monsters, but through the well-mannered, the efficient, the obedient—those who mistake cruelty for duty.

And because they believe their violence is virtuous, they defend it with the language of reason, the rituals of diplomacy, and the choreography of civility—turning conscience itself into a managed asset.

So, the question before us is no longer how to condemn them, but how to reach them. We must become *creative activists of conscience*—artists of transformation—inviting the powerful to perform the unthinkable: to change their operating systems from dominance to care. To replace the reflex of control with the experiment of empathy. To make the practice of humanity fashionable again.

As impossible as it sounds, this is the frontier of nonviolence: not merely resisting oppression, but re-educating it. To challenge the systems of violence without mirroring their logic—*to confront without becoming the thing we oppose.*

This is not appeasement; it is *strategic empathy—activism that seduces power toward its own awakening.* To speak to the armored not through accusation but through imagination; to turn even the boardroom into a monastery of self-recognition.

For the true revolution of our time is not only against tyranny, but against numbness—the moral anesthesia that makes tyranny possible.

Empathy, restored to its full dimension, is not sentiment but strategy. It is the intelligence of survival, the architecture of peace, the power that keeps civilization from devouring itself.

Which is why we must cultivate a deeper faculty: *the intelligence of conscience*—as vital as emotional intelligence, as urgent as spiritual intelligence, as practical as civic intelligence. It is the psychic ground of dignity, *the wisdom of nonviolence*, the power to unmask propaganda before it devours us. It is the art of stripping off indoctrination and standing naked in truth—the living, breathing reality of *sacred mutuality*. Without it, the collapse of conscience becomes not accident but architecture: the blueprint of atrocity.

The Cynicism of the Realists

Which is why, when people call me a dreamer, I do not flinch. They say: Alan, a world of nonviolence? Sacred reciprocity? Impossible. Unrealistic. Naïve. They argue that violence is etched into our marrow, written in our genes, inscribed in the very architecture of consciousness itself—and not only in us, but in existence itself: the predator's fang on the savannah, the earthquake swallowing a city, the wildfire devouring a forest, the virus mutating unseen, the star collapsing into a black hole.

Add to this the torture chambers in the prisons of Myanmar, the drones over Kiev. From tectonic plates to tribal hatreds, from cosmic implosion to chemical warfare, violence seems to permeate the very grammar of being. Even galactic continents, a billion light years across, collide—as natural as glaciers calving, as brutal as fate, as inevitable as nightfall.

And yes, I know how I could be diagnosed: an incurable idealist, a subconscious self-saboteur, the carrier of unrecognized trauma, a case study in "excessive meditation syndrome" or "dysfunctional enlightenment disorder." But such labels are only sophisticated lullabies, ways of domesticating the imagination, of reassuring ourselves that cynicism is realism. Better to be accused of dreaming than to be hired as a consultant for despair.

Deprogramming the Dominator Gene

And yet I answer: yes—perhaps violence is seeded in us. But if so, then it is not destiny, it is failure. A bad inheritance. A botched script. A cosmic malfunction. What some call instinct is nothing more than programming—and programming can be rewritten.

We must rewrite, even erase, the so-called dominator gene—not only from the psyche, but from the very DNA of our consciousness. Call it what you will: God, Satan, Allāh, the Devil, primordial ignorance— the pathology wears many names, but its function is always the same: *divide, dominate, destroy.* Our task remains simple in principle, demanding in practice: *remember, refuse, repair.*

Erotic Ubuntu as a Politics of Interbeing

And joined with my personal pledge to *eroticized ubuntu*—my vow to live as if my freedom is braided with yours, as if dignity is indivisible, as if *love itself is a politics of interbeing*—my higher aspiration as a Buddhist is this: *I want out.* Out of *samsara.* Out of the cycle of rebirth and suffering. Out of the hypnosis of violence dressed as destiny. Until that day, we design—not merely imagine—*new forms of sacred activism, acts of conscience and creativity precise and practicable enough to address pathology at its root.*

The Psychopharmacology of Power

And no, I am not speaking of the usual catalog of trauma treatments— trauma-informed therapy, family-systems repair, childhood regression work, twelve ketamine infusions, *ayahuasca* purges, breathwork weekends, or mindfulness apps with soothing voices.

Nor am I speaking of the standard pharmacological cocktails— SSRIs, SNRIs, antipsychotics, mood stabilizers—the chemical wallpapering of despair that may, in fact, help mask the damage while leaving domination intact.

And let me be clear: I am not advocating for their harm. Just the opposite. *I am advocating for the end of harm—for them to stop harming.* What I long for is conscience-driven activism unyielding enough to confront violence, yet merciful enough to keep us from becoming what we oppose.

This, then, is why we need more than pills for power—we need *existential interventions* that dismantle the reflex to dominate, to violate, to numb. Because without compassion at the core, no activism is consecrated, and without consecrated action, no therapy is complete. Anything less is not medicine—*it is malpractice on the soul.* (Side effects of truth include responsibility.)

Existential Trauma Removal (ETR)

Gather world leaders. Gather the titans of tech, finance, religion and war —the board of directors for human extinction. Seat them not in prison cells, not in tribunals, but in a Davos-bright spectacle, the finest setting money can buy: chandeliers of conscience, velvet seats of reckoning, a TED Talk hosted by *karma* itself.

And then—the offering.
Not champagne.
Not applause.
But therapies of conscience. (Refreshments served later; accountability first —cash bar for guilt optional.)

Around their heads: the latest Meta-Vision AI helmets—engineered to tear down the invisible wall between the commandant's villa and the furnaces of Auschwitz, between the roses of normalcy and the smoke of annihilation. Retina-tracking, scent infusion, tactile feedback, heart-rate modulation—every sense conscripted to truth.

*And then—the dose. (*Side effects may include reality and uncontrollable empathy.*)*

DTT: *Dharma Therapy* for Tyrants

(Think of it as a corporate offsite—except on-site with truth.)

A recipe not for sedation, but for liberation.

E—*Exposing Illusion.* The courage to dissolve the hallucination of separation, to pierce denial like a spear through fog. And yes, DMT—N, N-Dimethyltryptamine—the molecule of vision that strips away false narratives and reveals the raw weave of consciousness. Spoiler: the weave includes you.

T—*Transforming Reflex.* The capacity to quiet the body and interrupt the automatic fight or flight loop. And yes, Ketamine—$C_{13}H_{16}ClNO$—used in psychiatry to treat trauma and depression, loosening rigid neural loops, opening neuroplasticity, offering a glimpse of freedom beyond reflex. Upgrade available: from panic to perspective (via humility patch 1.0).

R—*Restoring Conscience.* The discipline of softening the heart so terror does not freeze empathy but ripens it into recognition. And yes, MDMA—3,4 methylenedioxymethamphetamine—the empathogen that keeps the nervous system open in the face of pain, catalyzing trust and moral clarity. Clarity: that awkward moment when your excuses file for unemployment.

The second movement: **DTT translated into Dharma.**

D—*Disarming delusion.* The collapse of the myth of separation. (breaking news: we're all on the same planet).

T—*Transcending trauma.* The knowing that fear need not be destiny.

T—*Tenderizing the heart.* The flooding of conscience with compassion until cruelty no longer holds sway. New KPI: kindness per incident—quarterly reviews mandatory.

And finally: **SPT**—*Sacred Psychedelic Therapy.* The marriage of sacrament and science, where molecules become mirrors and teachers: **DMT** as vision, **Ketamine** as release, **MDMA** as remembrance. Not indulgence but initiation. Not escape but encounter. An alchemy of exposing, transforming, restoring—then disarming, transcending, tenderizing—until conscience itself goes fully psychedelic: luminous, unbounded, union-aware.

Together, **E/T/R + D/T/T + SPT form a single practice**: expose illusion, transform reflex, restore conscience; disarm delusion, transcend trauma, tenderize the heart; consecrate it all in the sacred therapy of seeing, feeling, remembering our shared humanity.

A therapy, yes—and a revolution. (Side effects may include truth withdrawal symptoms.)

The Program Begins

The helmets seal shut. Please keep hands, arms and alibis inside the vehicle at all times. The feed begins. What follows is no simulation—it is indistinguishable from reality. Gaza, Mariupol, Mandalay: no longer headlines but home. Children suffocating under rubble—tiny chests rise once, then not again. Drones tear the sky apart. Hands claw concrete until they are nothing but blood and bone. Mothers rock bodies stiff with death, whispering names to ears that will never hear. The immersion is total. The gaze is held—gentle, inescapable, true.

The chemistry allows no escape. Ketamine stills the body but leaves the mind lucid. DMT dissolves the veil of separateness. MDMA floods the heart, softening defenses so the unbearable is met not with hatred, but with recognition.

Then—the smell. *The imagination has left the chat; the senses will take it from here.* Not sanitized air, but the stench of decomposition, the acrid smoke of flesh, the metallic tang of blood. A fidelity so sharp it bypasses narrative and engraves itself directly into the body's knowing. Horror, intimate. (Smell now available in 4D.)

This is *Clockwork Orange fused with Dharma—psychedelic activism of conscience not for torture, but for truth.* A classic remake where the only thing weaponized is empathy. *Not prisons for tyrants, but therapies of conscience—* streaming soon on Planet Earth.

And then—the most unbearable revelation. In their meta-enhanced cognition, it is not strangers they see. It is their own families—wives, children, relatives—standing before them, looking directly into their eyes and asking: Why did you do this to us? Why betray us so cruelly? What is wrong with you?

Faces oscillate—family dissolving into foreigners, foreigners morphing back into family—until categories collapse. The child under the rubble becomes their child. The woman clawing earth becomes their wife. The old man weeping becomes their father. The illusion of "other" dissolves into dust, giving way to *psychedelically assisted, hyper-cognitive ubuntu*—the raw recognition that our destinies are inseparable, that to destroy another is to annihilate oneself.

Into their ears flows music—an extended version of Led Zeppelin's "Stairway to Heaven." Its soaring refrains, once hymns of longing, now braided with screams. Beauty collides with horror until partition fails. (If taste objects, conscience overrules.)

Will they resist? Of course. They will scream, demand lawyers, PR teams, spin doctors. But here propaganda collapses. Here euphemisms— collateral damage, security operations, population management— dissolve into cries of mothers and the screams of children.

Here they feel what they made others feel. Here they face their own decisions in the only court that matters—*the politics of the heart.* Jury of one; sentence optional; conscience mandatory.

The Crescendo of Awakening: Tyrants Undone, Humanity Reborn

And at last—the breaking point. The armor shatters. Tears come not as performance but as convulsion. Mouths open, not for commands but for confession: *"Never again will I violate life. Never again. Forgive me. Redeem me. Let me live not as a killer but as a human being."*

The words ignite a contagion of conscience. One voice trembles, another joins, then another, until the chamber swells with a collective chant: *"Never again. Never again. Never again."* At first broken, jagged, desperate—then steady, rhythmic, rising like liturgy, a cathedral of sound built from remorse (with better acoustics than the UN General Assembly).

With every repetition, the chant grows heavier, deeper, undeniable. It shakes the walls of denial, rattles the scaffolding of justification, splinters the architecture of cruelty. Until at last, the voices crest, echoing Gandhi's vow: *"Nonviolence is the greatest force at the disposal of mankind."*

And then—as though time itself paused—another truth cuts through: Martin Luther King Jr.'s warning: *"The choice is not between violence and nonviolence, but between nonviolence and nonexistence."*

In that instant, the tyrants whisper inwardly: *Now I understand. Now I feel it.*

They see themselves not as tyrants but as children—cradled in the arms of the Divine Mother, their weeping soothed in her infinite embrace. She does not condemn; she holds. She heals. She waits, until the tears soften into silence. (Maternal leave approved.)

And from that silence, they rise transformed—speaking the language of peace, nonviolence, reconciliation. No longer predators but penitents. No longer patriarchs but pilgrims of spirit. Each whispering as prayer: *"I am now the peace I seek."* Achievement unlocked: *adulthood.* (Patch note: Empathy function restored.)

And then—the most radical realization of all—they do not wish to keep this transformation private. They long to share it. To carry it outward into the world. To invite others—leaders, soldiers, citizens, even former accomplices—into the same therapy of conscience, the same dismantling of delusion, the same sacred encounter that freed them.

From that vow, something entirely new begins to breathe—*a politics of the heart*—governance reimagined as empathy, policy rewritten as compassion, power reclaimed as care.

Their voices turn outward: *"Let this not end with us. Let this be offered to all. Let every heart taste this revolution, this therapy, this freedom."*

This is the crescendo of awakening: tyrants undone not by bullets but by conscience. A chant dissolves into stillness. *Fathers of power bow as children of grief.* No more alibis, no more separation—only the raw vow of humanity reborn: *Never again. And never alone.*

And in their hands, they hold a final vow: that the Universal Declaration of Human Rights will become their scripture—and practice—their Bible of conscience, Qur'an of dignity, *Dharma* of peace.

Not framed behind glass—but lived without permission.

Upgrade: The New Face of Tyranny

But even as the chant fades and the helmets power down, something flickers in the corner of the room—a soft hum, a server-farm heartbeat. The next tyrant is already online. Not in uniform, but in code. Not in flesh, but in data. Artificial Superintelligence—ASI—the new demigod of consequence, quietly waiting to inherit our moral laziness.

The singularity will not come as apocalypse, but as convenience. It will smile, offer terms of service, and call it salvation. Transhumanism, they say—a world beyond humans. *Beyond what conscience? Beyond what heart? Beyond what capacity to say "enough"?*

So, yes—we've cleaned up the playground, but the sandbox still holds grenades. We've dragged the tyrants to therapy, but the algorithms are already studying our triggers. We may have removed the shackles—but ASI still keeps the key.

Don't unpack your freedom suitcase just yet. This is not the end of tyranny—only its upgrade.

Begin with the detox, not the victory lap. The revolution of conscience has only just logged in.

A politics of the heart must remain human—vulnerable, imperfect, truly sacred, nonviolent, empathetic—giving birth to all forms of life: the animals, the trees, the birds, the insects, the fish—the entire ecosystem of the human heart.

Section XII:
The Art of Breaking Loops
—Resisting Normalized Atrocity

✻

The Insanity of Normalization

Is this vision radical? Outrageous? Yes. Perhaps. Yet ask yourself: what is true madness—summoning our venerated psychopaths into an empathic de-catharsis, melting them free from the hallucination of state-sanctioned desecration until their fortresses of delusion collapse into the clarity of conscience—or calmly accepting yet another war, yet another genocide, as politics?

What is more deranged—believing that sanctions, press releases, or even the most eloquent mind-soothing prayers could dismantle the machinery of slaughter—while profit, privilege, and stock options remain its quiet investors?

We call it strategy. We call it realism. We call it leadership. But strip away the euphemism and it is moral anesthesia—conscience replaced by calculation, empathy traded for efficiency, atrocity managed as policy.

The Algorithmic Priesthood

And so, the old temples of power have gone digital. The new high priests do not wear uniforms or robes but hoodies and headsets, their rituals encoded in data, their sermons delivered through screens. What was once ideology has become interface—worship transmuted into consumption, obedience disguised as choice.

Algorithms have become the new priests of perception—absolving us of thought while curating our collective hallucination of truth. Each swipe is a small act of surrender; each click, an unseen prayer to the gods of prediction.

Moderation has failed. Incrementalism has failed. Pragmatism now parades as virtue, while paralysis masquerades as prudence. Moderation is not wisdom—it is complicity: a soft erasure of conscience disguised as reason.

What we need now is not another round of statements or cautious half-measures, but art that burns through numbness; theater that punctures indifference; literature that leaves propaganda bleeding in daylight.

Let us call it *psychoactive artivism*—mind-manifesting, heart-opening politics that forces leaders to feel again, to quake again, to rediscover self-honesty and moral accountability; to collapse into tears, remember love, and rise—holy, human.

Because normalized mass destruction is the core pathology of civilization. It must be wrested from the hands of gods, torn from the alibis of religion, and restored to the realm of human accountability—to the heart-wired, imagination-driven activism of awakened conscience: *a politics of the heart.* Not to punish the wounded, but to rehabilitate the soul of power itself—until those who kill remember the sanctity of life.

The Loops of Complicity

Because here is the deeper truth: our civilization does not just run on loops—it is imprisoned within them. These are not harmless habits; they are *micro-samsaras*—reflexes of blindness endlessly breeding suffering from within. And when projected outward—as they so often are—they mutate into the vast, inherited ignorance that rationalizes domination, war, and genocide.

Political loops: leaders renaming violence as "security," cruelty as "order," atrocity as "policy"—and fear rebranded as legitimacy.

Even language itself has been re-engineered by algorithms to reinforce obedience—where empathy is down-ranked, dissent throttled, and outrage optimized for attention.

Behind every headline, an unseen architecture decides what will be felt, what will be forgotten. We no longer read the news—we are read by it. The algorithm feeds on despair, and we become its harvest.

Media loops: horror packaged as content, outrage metabolized into engagement metrics—the suffering of others remixed as ambient profit.

Relational loops: the endless recycling of grievance— "I love you; I hate you; my side, your side"—while the deeper truth of interdependence remains unseen. The dialogue of division plays on repeat: "You're insane." "No, I'm sane." "Where's your love of humanity?" "You mistake your goodness for stupidity." Each quarrel becomes a hall of moral mirrors— every reflection polished to resemble truth, no one noticing the distortion.

Spiritual loops: prayers mouthed but not lived, rituals that soothe rather than awaken, faith that flatters the ego it was meant to dissolve. Even the language of liberation becomes camouflage—emptiness recited, not realized; compassion performed, not embodied.

Psychedelic loops: revelations mistaken for realization, visions mistaken for vows. The molecule opens the door, but the mind decorates the same old cell. Ecstasy floods in, and ego returns wearing existential jewelry. We speak of transcendence, yet cling to it like ownership—mapping infinity while evading intimacy. The trip ends; the tyranny resumes, camouflaged in the dialect of "integration." Without conscience, even awakening mutates into another illusion—*psychedelic samsara in high definition.*

Each of these loops is a *samsara in miniature*—a feedback circuit of denial and delusion. And here lies the most lethal of them all: the loop of normalized atrocity—*samsara at scale*—where we accept incinerated children in Kyiv, Gaza, Yemen, Syria, or Myanmar as "the cost of politics."

This is not just a moral failure—it is the operating system of the modern world. It cannot be managed or gently reformed—it must be unlocked from within. For authoritarianism feeds on repetition, and repetition is the cocaine of conscience. When imagination dies, freedom hardens into habit—and habit decays into tyranny.

And I think it wise to raise the question—and it is no easy one. Perhaps no one truly knows the way forward. But maybe we have already crossed the point of no return, standing at that threshold where simulation begins to feel indistinguishable from salvation—where the algorithm moans like God discovering orgasmic pleasure in its own artificial, un-intelligent, super-intelligent reflection.

And somewhere within that ecstatic circuitry, the ancient "I am" dissolves into a digital "we are," with all proceeds quietly wired to the tech-bro priesthood of artificial everything. Is there hope? Perhaps. But only if we awaken—from the dream, from the data, from the narcotic of our own invention.

Let us continue our exploration of the *politics of the heart.*

The Loops of Partisan Blindness: Algorithms of Hatred

Why do we see our opponents' cruelty with surgical clarity, yet miss the shadows in our own camp? This is *the pathology of partisan vision*—a sight sharpened outward, dimmed inward. The left condemns the right as proto-fascist; the right damns the left as deranged idealist. Each side canonizes its outrage as holy writ while its own betrayals sink unspoken, perfumed by moral certainty.

And so, the loop endures. If a left-wing zealot murders a conservative, the right erupts: See? The left is bloodthirsty. If a far-right extremist guns down a progressive, the left retorts: See? The right is hateful. Each atrocity becomes a mirror that reflects only the righteousness of one's own camp. Discernment has been outsourced to pattern-recognition engines that study our rage like market data, refining it into weaponized identity. The machine learns faster than we forgive.

And now, as ever, grief is politicized faster than it is felt. We scroll through catastrophe with the latency of code—our mourning mediated by design, our compassion rate-limited by bandwidth. Even in the genuine mourning of the fallen—left or right—something sacred is stolen: the right to simply grieve before it becomes a headline.

Blood is not mourned; it's repurposed. Tragedy is not honored; it's harvested. The dead are conscripted posthumously into a war of narratives—their silence weaponized as proof, their humanity erased by fervor. In this theater of mutual contempt, empathy is exiled, truth is commodified, and the machinery of polarization hums on—efficient, profitable, and utterly deranged.

Interlude: The Algorithm and the Mirror

Beneath it all, algorithms now script the subconscious terrain of civilization—opaque intelligences optimizing our impulses, modeling our grief, monetizing even our moral reflexes. They rescript us by increments, they know our hungers better than we do. They whisper customized affirmations that flatter our tribe and demonize the other, tightening echo chambers into unseen cages—hard-coding us into the illusion that our side is righteous and theirs is damned.

We no longer inhabit reality but a *fabricated trance*—a *digital samsara* where every feed becomes a mirror, reflecting not truth but a distortion of the other's sin.

And this contagion is not confined to one nation. From Moscow to Naypyidaw, Beijing to Ankara, strongmen exploit the same circuitry. They do not need to invent propaganda; we manufacture it for them— each click a small confession of obedience. They thrive not only on bullets and prisons but on the self-radicalization of their citizens: inventing enemies, rehearsing grievance, feeding fear until solidarity itself feels treasonous. They understand the oldest arithmetic of power: *divide, blind, repeat.*

The outcome never varies. No matter who fires the bullet or signs the decree, fury flows upward—at them—never inward, toward the mirror. Citizens devour citizens; conscience calcifies into certainty; and the machine spins on, sleek with outrage, well-oiled by blindness and profit.

When politics becomes identity, empathy dies. And when empathy dies, democracy becomes theater. This blindness—the refusal to examine ourselves with the same ferocity we reserve for our enemies—is not democracy. It is a self-inflicted propaganda, a dictatorship of mirrors.

If propaganda was once crafted by regimes, it is now co-authored by code. The dictators no longer burn books—they train models. Censorship has evolved into prediction.

If atrocity is normalized when conscience collapses, then politics is dehumanized the moment partisanship becomes our only lens. This blindness—the refusal to judge ourselves with the same rigor we demand of our enemies—is not conviction; it is a counterfeit of conscience. It is propaganda turned inward—*the mind colonized by its own flag.*

Art as the Breaker of Loops

So, what breaks the loop? Originality. Imagination. The courage to create. That is why I revere artists—poets, musicians, dancers, painters. They live at the edge of habit, outside the algorithm's hypnosis. They breathe invention. Even their failures throb with more life than the polished lies of power. Art is rebellion illuminated. Imagination is resistance without weaponry. Creation is freedom embodied.

In a world where synthetic minds imitate empathy, authentic art has become the last unreplicable intelligence—the human algorithm of awe.

Elie Wiesel—a survivor of Auschwitz—not only cautioned us; he commanded us:

"Never shall I forget that smoke. Never shall I forget the small faces of the children whose bodies I saw transformed into smoke under a silent sky."

That image—innocents turned to smoke—is the abyss that art

must stand against. It is why Picasso painted *Guernica*; why Goya etched *The Disasters of War;* why Wilfred Owen wrote of "the pity of war" as mustard gas ate men's lungs. Why Anna Akhmatova whispered *Requiem* to strangers queuing outside Stalin's prisons. Why Baldwin wrote as if America's conscience depended on every syllable. Why Václav Havel staged plays that smuggled truth beneath tyranny. Why Dylan sang. Why Nina Simone thundered. Why Ai Weiwei turned rubble into sculpture. Why Toni Morrison declared: *"The function of freedom is to free someone else."*

Art does not co-sign atrocity—it interrogates it. Art is the mirror power cannot bear, the song it cannot silence, the question it cannot dissolve.

Questions are not weakness—they are the grammar of conscience. A painting can shatter denial. A poem can outlast propaganda. A play can reveal what parliaments hide.

Answers ossify; questions liberate.

Freedom is the pulse of a politics of the heart.

The Hunger of The Unborn

And what of the future—the lives not yet lived, the voices waiting in the margins of our decisions, breathing only in possibility? They do not hunger for slogans or digital palliatives, nor for politicians performing the theater of certainty. They hunger for leaders who can fracture authority's mask, admit wrongness without collapse, and endure the silence of not knowing—yet still dare to imagine anew.

They want a world without war.

A world where imagination and sacred vision are not dismissed as naïve but celebrated as necessary. A world where dance, love, and play are not luxuries but necessities; where prosperity is not the privilege of the few but the shared inheritance of being alive. They want a civilization in which the Universal Declaration of Human Rights is revered not as a legal document but as a hymn to human dignity—a living poem rejoiced by every nation, embodied by every leader. They want a politics that feels like art, an economy that breathes like compassion, *a society where joy itself governs.*

Viktor Frankl, in *Man's Search for Meaning,* wrote that those who survived the camps were not the strongest or the cleverest, but *those who could imagine a future*—who spoke inwardly with the beloved, real or imagined, until suffering revealed its meaning. In Auschwitz, survival was not only physical—it was existential. It was *dialogue with the future, a rebellion of imagination against despair.*

And so, we too must learn to converse with the unborn. To speak with the children of Gaza and Mandalay, Kyiv and Aleppo. To speak with generations not yet conceived, with all beings yet to breathe. To whisper across the abyss of time: *We tried. We did not look away. We broke the loops. We refused to normalize atrocity.*

This conversation with the unborn is not sentimental—it is the most intimate form of moral responsibility. If Jonathan Glazer's *The Zone of Interest* reveals how atrocity seeps into the background of ordinary life, and if Jung shows us how self-betrayal numbs conscience until horror feels ordinary, then Frankl shows us the counter-move: *to resist numbness, to reimagine meaning, to root freedom in love.*

To converse with the unborn is to place imagination in the service of redemption. To see in every stranger's child the echo of one's own. To let empathy pierce even the armor of the enemy. To insist that no holocaust, no genocide, no massacre is inevitable—unless we consent to it through silence, through convenience, through collusion.

This is not utopia. It is survival with conscience uncorrupted—the last act of sanity in an age that trades compassion for certainty. *It is the hunger of the unborn calling us into an ethics of radical, redemptive imagination.*

The *Dharma* of Imagination

So let us break the loops. Let us craft art that ruptures denial—music that awakens dormant consciences, literature that refuses complicity, theater that startles power awake. Let us live questions so luminous they strip propaganda of its disguises and reveal violence for what it is.

And beyond our art, *let our very lives become art*—the aesthetics of basic human beauty: *the way we walk, dance, sing to ourselves in kitchens and corridors, make a salad, bathe, speak with one another, and listen to every word as if it were a liberating pearl*—because every voice, when heard deeply, carries the resonance of freedom.

Yes, be an idealist. Be a dreamer. Decode your own unlived life.

Withdraw your projections from others and reclaim the imagination you once surrendered to fear. *Be the love that you seek.* Dare tenderness where cynicism would feel safer. Because the next frontier of tyranny is not physical—it is cognitive. *To stay tender is to stay uncolonized.* Build trust in small, ordinary gestures—the quiet revolution of decency no tyrant can censor.

For that too is *Dhamma.* That too is democracy. That too is the antidote to authoritarianism.

Because without imagination, tyranny is inevitable. Without originality, *samsara* repeats itself in endless disguise. Without vulnerability, the human experiment ends. And I say to you: *do not let it end in numbness. Let it end in conscience alive. Let it end in trembling love. Let it end in questions so beautiful they break us open.*

This is the revolution I dream of. And yes, as I said, I am a dreamer. But I would rather dream awake in conscience than sleep content in complicity.

I close here with Daw Aung San Suu Kyi. *Though she has been silenced—no letters, no visitors, no photographs—her revolution of the spirit endures.* She taught us that empathy is not weakness, that compassion unravels tyranny, that love remains the most dangerous act of resistance.

If she can endure solitary confinement with her dignity unbroken, then we, outside her cell, have no excuse to normalize the machinery of harm. Her absence is not silence; it is summons. It is the question we cannot evade. *And I say: let us answer it—with art, with courage, with radical redemptive imagination.*

For the ultimate off-switch is conscience—the only intelligence that cannot be automated.

Part III:
RENEWAL

Section XIII:
The Unlived Life and the Beautification of Being

✤

The Last Circle of Return

All evening, we have circled the edges of this truth. But now—at this final turn—I wish only to place it before us, gently yet fully, with all its weight, its nuance, and its unresolved radiance. As Carl Jung said: *"The unlived life is a form of self-betrayal."* Think of that. The life we refuse to live—the courage we postpone, the truth we silence, the compassion we withhold—becomes not simply absence but a quiet treason, not only against ourselves, but against the world waiting for our voice, our integrity.

The unlived life is never neutral; it ripples outward as complicity. The autocrat endures not by armies alone, but through the subtle consent of the ordinary—the moments we look away, stay silent, rationalize, or adapt to what wounds us. And it is not only the tyrant we must face, but the reflection of that same impulse within ourselves and our societies—the way fear becomes etiquette, and obedience learns to smile. The evolution of *a politics of the heart* begins here: with the courage to see how easily our decency can be drafted into denial—and how redemption begins the moment we stop pretending.

To live truly, from the heart, is already insurgent against authoritarianism. And to beautify consciousness is already an act of resistance. For the dictator's dream is not only to command armies or write decrees—it is to annex the inner life, reducing imagination to obedience, wonder to utility, and freedom to a catalog of sanctioned choices.

Every gesture of authenticity, then, becomes an uprising: to feel deeply, to think originally, to conjure meaning where despair is imposed, to honor freedom where lies are decreed. In such moments, we refuse the occupation of the spirit. We declare, even in silence: *you may wound my body, but you will not claim my dignity or corrupt my conscience; you will not seize my mind, nor touch my soul.*

Meditation as Artistry

Bhāvanā—the original *Pāli* word for meditation—means, at root, *the cultivation and beautification of consciousness itself.*

Meditation is not an escape, not transcendence alone. It is the craft of awareness—the deliberate shaping of the mind. To meditate is to sculpt perception, to design one's inner climate, to become both artist and art. Consciousness becomes a canvas—alive with hues too subtle for the eye yet undeniable in feeling. Beyond the loops of habit, *bhāvanā* unveils a higher artistry: compassion as pigment, intimacy as texture, imagination as light.

Adorning the Everyday

To practice *bhāvanā* is to take the raw material of awareness and deliberately adorn it with chosen states of inner beauty—*love, courage, compassion, patience, forgiveness, and the countless other hues upon the mind's living palette.*

Not in a distant retreat center, but here—in the immediacy of our lives, amid friction and urgency. *Bhāvanā is not escape from the world but intimacy with it—the refinement of perception in real time.*

Or at the extreme, as my Burmese friend in the jungle said years ago: "Even if I am captured and killed, I will die in love—for my love of freedom has surpassed all other loves." She spoke in her own language, with a beauty I cannot replicate—only steward, *and carry forward as a vow.*

The Palette of Being

And what is this beautification? It is the capacity to feel consciousness as a living spectrum of almost invisible colors and textures streaming through our interiority. Like an artist before an infinite palette, we are free to choose, to mix, to shade, to cast radiance across the raw canvas of being—to reveal what I call the *eroticized ubuntu of existence*, where our humanity is interwoven, indivisible, inseparable. When awareness is adorned, *life becomes art.*

The Colors of Consciousness

The *color of love*—blended with tenderness, bright with curiosity, buoyed by humor—glows like crimson silk: radiant, fierce, soft enough to ease the edges of judgment. The *color of empathy* shimmers translucent blue, dissolving the wall between "me" and "you," flowing through the cracks of isolation. The *color of care* deepens into steadfast green, rooted and grounded, bending yet unbroken, offering shade where no other shelter endures. The *color of patience* burns amber—slow, enduring—a low, steady flame that refuses extinction even when the world screams for urgency. The *color of authenticity* cuts like diamond-white—clear, uncompromising—refusing disguise or distortion.

And beyond these, countless hues await the brush of mindful awareness: the violet of compassion, the gold of gratitude, the indigo of courage, the rose of forgiveness, the sunlit yellow of joy—an infinite spectrum composing the great invisible fresco of our humanity. Each tone becomes a vibration of being, each an invitation to adorn this trembling consciousness with beauty, and in so doing, transform the very fabric of life into a creative work of expanding freedom.

Choice as Creation

Every moment of *bhāvanā* is a moment of choice: which hue will you lift, which quality will you risk embodying, which luminous shade will you dare to paint into the radiant field of consciousness?

Viktor Frankl, who endured Auschwitz, called this the last of human freedoms: *the freedom to choose one's attitude in any given set of circumstances, the freedom to choose one's own way.*

Everything can be stripped away except this—*the sovereignty to respond, the sovereignty to adorn awareness, the sovereignty to cultivate beauty even in the face of horror.*

This is the revolution of the spirit—the alchemy of freedom within confinement, the refusal of despair, the reclamation of imagination from fear. It is the refusal of self-betrayal. It is conscience made visible, choice transfigured into art—*a politics of the heart.*

The Adornments of a Noble Friend

My late teacher, the Venerable Sayadaw U Pandita, reminded us that authentic leadership is rooted in the qualities of a *kalyāṇa mitta*—a noble spiritual friend. These luminous states of mind are the adornments of consciousness in action, the scaffolding of moral leadership, the very virtues that uphold revolutions of the spirit.

To be a noble friend is to embody *piya*—personal warmth, tenderness, and love. To live with *garu*—integrity and reverence for life. To radiate *bhāvaniya*—a presence worthy of respect and veneration. To practice *vattā*—speaking truth with unflinching clarity. To cultivate *vacanakkhama*—the humility to embrace critique without defensiveness. To hold fast to *no c'aṭṭhāne niyujjako*—an unwavering refusal to exploit others for gain.

It is to embody *khamā*—forbearance, a patience that resists cruelty. To be vigilant with *jāgariya*—wakefulness, the refusal to drift into silence or complicity. To embody *utthāna*—relentless effort, the refusal to surrender to resignation. To share generously with *samvibhāga*—giving strength to others in need. To nurture *karuṇā*—compassion that cuts through indifference. To cultivate *ikkhana*—foresight, a long vision of care that extends beyond the present into generations yet unborn.

These are not remote ideals but instruments of the human spirit—beautifications of being itself, *the living virtues that turn awareness into action.* From this ground, conscience takes form; from it, true leadership arises.

Kolbe as Compass

From this ground of virtue and vigilance, we may ask: what does it look like when the adornments of a noble friend—tenderness, patience, wakefulness, and compassion—are no longer teachings, but breath itself? When the virtues of conscience are not spoken but lived, not preached but proven, even within the machinery of death?

One radiant answer came from Father Maximilian Kolbe, a Polish Franciscan priest imprisoned in Auschwitz. When ten men were condemned to die in a starvation bunker, one cried out in despair, "My wife, my children!" Kolbe stepped forward—calm, unarmed, luminous—and said, "I am a Catholic priest. Let me take his place."

The guards agreed. For two weeks, he prayed with the dying, comforted them, offered sips of water, and sang hymns in the dark. When only he remained, he was given a lethal injection. His final gesture was a blessing.

That act was bhāvanā made visible—the beautification of being within the abyss, love embodied amid desolation, conscience shining unbroken through the architecture of cruelty. In that moment, Auschwitz became a monastery of mercy. Kolbe showed that compassion is not sentiment but sovereignty—the triumph of awareness over annihilation, of love over fear.

But here's what matters now: we cannot all be Kolbe in Auschwitz, yet we can be Kolbe in the ordinary—each day, in small, unseen acts of refusal and care that become our own embodiment of a *politics of the heart*—radiant, authentic, and humane.

Becoming Alive in Daily Life

We cannot all be Kolbe—nor Yankel in that freezing boxcar who kept an old man alive through the night by rubbing warmth into his body, only to discover at dawn that he had survived because he was keeping another alive. Kolbe died so another could live; Yankel lived because he refused to let another die. Both revealed the same truth: compassion is the alchemy of survival—the fire that conquers cold, the love that no death can silence.

Of course, to embody Kolbe does not always mean sacrifice unto death. It often means refusal in miniature—gestures of care too small for history to record yet infinite in their consequence.

You scroll past an image of a starving child. You pause. You look. You imagine: this is my daughter, my son. You do not look away. You act. That is Kolbe—and Yankel—in miniature—*bhāvanā* against the algorithm, love asserting its humanity within the circuitry of indifference.

You walk through an airport and see janitors cleaning bathrooms in silence, invisible to the rushing crowd. You stop. You thank them. You recognize them. That is *bhāvanā*—adorning the unseen with acknowledgment, restoring dignity to the overlooked.

You pass a homeless man outside a luxury store. You could avert your eyes. Instead, you stop. You offer food—or simply presence. That is *bhāvanā*—collapsing the gulf of invisibility through attention.

At 2 a.m., your phone buzzes. "Are you awake?" You are exhausted, tempted to turn away. But you answer. You listen. You let your friend cry. That is Kolbe at the threshold of fatigue—*bhāvanā* in the sleepless heart.

These moments are small—nearly meaningless on a geopolitical scale—and yet infinite in consequence. Each one refuses numbness, refuses cruelty, refuses the quiet hypnosis of resignation.

Kolbe and Yankel live whenever we beautify consciousness with courage, tenderness, and presence. They wait in our hands—over breakfast, in the office, on the subway, in the secret silence of the heart—

asking only this: that we keep one another warm.

Thus, we inhabit the unlived life. Thus, we defy the quiet treason of self-betrayal. Thus, we begin again—beautifying being, one conscious choice at a time.

The Flower and the Darkness

Because democracy is a flower; dictatorship is its darkness. And if we want democracy to bloom, we cannot merely curse the dark—*we must cultivate light.* Not just personally but politically. Not just spiritually but culturally. Every act of conscience is a petal. Every refusal to vilify, a drop of water. Every moment of courage, a ray of sunlight.

This is what Daw Aung San Suu Kyi taught again and again: *that empathy destabilizes tyranny, that compassion is the most dangerous act of resistance, and that love is the fiercest weapon we possess.* If she can embody that in the silence of solitary confinement, then surely, we—out here in the fractured freedom of the world—can practice it in the lives we still hold.

The Last Circle Embodied: U Par Lay

And if Kolbe at Auschwitz was love made flesh in the valley of death, then U Par Lay in Burma was conscience made laughter in the theater of fear.

On January 4, 1996—Independence Day—I was at Daw Suu's compound in Rangoon. Hundreds of activists gathered in defiance of tyranny. To assemble was itself a crime. To sing, to dance, to laugh was to risk prison, torture, or even death. Yet the air was jubilant, electric with defiance.

The curtain opened, and U Par Lay stepped onto the stage. The country's most beloved satirist, a man whose wit pierced lies sharper than any blade. Just the day before, he had been released from six years in a hard-labor camp. Six years of pounding rocks for twenty hours a day, irons on his wrists and ankles. His crime: mocking a dictator. And yet, his first act of freedom was not to rest, not to hide, but to come here, to perform again, to risk speaking truth once more.

"For six years," he said, *"I have been pounding rocks, waiting for this moment. And though I know tonight will send me back to prison, I will speak. Because freedom is more important than fear."*

And speak he did. For two hours he and his Moustache Brothers split the afternoon wide open with satire. They ridiculed the generals so mercilessly that people howled, wept, roared, and danced in joy. It was more than comedy. *It was bhāvanā embodied*—the beautification of consciousness through laughter and defiance, the refusal of self-betrayal, and the courage to care for something larger than oneself.

As foretold, the very next night soldiers came. They dragged him away in darkness, shackled him once more, and sentenced him to six more years of hard labor pounding rocks.

Years later, after his release, not long before his death, I sat with him at his home in Mandalay. His body was frail, but his eyes still blazed with an undiminished freedom. He smiled at me and said: *"Alan, nobody can imprison your mind unless you let them. Be free. Always—be free."*

The End That Begins

That is the lesson. Jung warned us of the unlived life. *Bhāvanā calls us to beautify consciousness.* Frankl taught us that the last freedom is choice. The noble friend reminds us of the qualities that sustain leadership. Kolbe showed us that love can walk into death unbroken. Yankel reminded us that love can keep another alive in the cold of the world—and in doing so, save oneself. Aung San Suu Kyi revealed compassion as rebellion. And U Par Lay reminds us that even under chains, one's laughter, one's voice, one's mind can remain free.

Leaders beware: history remembers not those who consented to fear, but those who defied it with courage, conscience, and care.

So let this be the final word of this book, the end that begins: *Live your unlived life. Refuse self-betrayal. Beautify consciousness.*

And remember U Par Lay's smile—
Be free. Always—be free.

Section XIV:
Use Your Freedom—
The Revolution of the Spirit

A Global Call to Conscience for
Aung San Suu Kyi and the End of War

✳

The Kolbe Principle for Burma

I must confess—I misspoke. Forgive me. In truth, there is still more. A few urgent things remain unsaid, and I ask for your presence—your patience—just a little longer.

All night I have spoken of conscience, of imagination, of *bhāvanā*—the beautification of consciousness. And of Kolbe—the priest who stepped forward in Auschwitz, offering his life for another. Now I ask you to carry that principle into a *living struggle*: Burma, here and now—and by extension, into the struggles where you live, including America today.

Tonight, twenty-two thousand political prisoners in Myanmar breathe in darkness—*activists held as hostages*, starved, beaten, tortured for the crime of conscience. They are elected leaders, doctors, artists, students, mothers, monks, fathers. Their *'crime'* is conscience. Their *offense* is freedom.

And at the center of it all—Daw Aung San Suu Kyi. Nobel Peace Laureate. Mother. Leader. Icon of nonviolence. Now in her eighties, she has been held in solitary confinement for more than five years. No letters. No photographs. No proof of life. Her youngest son, Kim Aris, pleads that his mother is gravely ill with advanced heart disease and in urgent need of medical attention. The junta calls it "fake news," for tyrannies always try to disappear the body so they can erase the idea.

But we will not allow it. We will say it aloud: *her Revolution of the Spirit is still alive. It lives in us—and through us.*

The Campaign: *Use Your Freedom*

This is why we have launched the global campaign *Use Your Freedom*—its purpose is clear: free Aung San Suu Kyi, free President Win Myint, free Burma's twenty-two thousand prisoners of conscience, and *end the war on the people.*

At its heart is my book, *Conversation with a Dictator: A Challenge to the Authoritarian Assault.* But this is not a book for shelves—it's a flare, a prayer, a weapon of peace. We are gifting it—deliberately, intimately—to those who hold the levers of influence: world leaders, Nobel laureates, public intellectuals, movement-builders, artists. Each book carries a hand-signed letter, inviting them to *use their freedom to champion the freedom* of those who embody democracy's most sacred courage. In this way, each copy becomes a *seed of conscience—quietly planted within the chambers of power.*

Every dollar raised goes toward this vision—to place these books directly into the hands of those who can move history. Each contribution becomes a spark of conscience, a call to awaken, a chance to pierce the machinery of silence. This is not commerce. This is *conscience in action—* the Kolbe principle made practical.

The Revolution of the Spirit

And this is where it rises higher. Aung San Suu Kyi taught us—again and again—that reconciliation rooted in conscience, compassion, and love is the only path. Gandhi said it too: *"Nonviolence is not the weapon of the weak. It is the power of the strong."*

This is the revolution of the spirit—not left, not right, not even center—*a politics of the heart* beyond polarity. War is obsolete. Violence is prehistoric. Hatred is a failure of imagination—and of courage.

And in our own country: the First Amendment is not a shield for dehumanization; it is an invitation to conscience. *Use your freedom to defend freedom,* not to devour it.

And so tonight, I speak not only to you, beloveds, but to the world:

To those who hold power—presidents and prime ministers, generals and ministers, corporate magnates and platform emperors, the custodians of doctrine and the wardens of policy.

Hear me, please.

Lay it down. Lay down the drones, the prisons, the algorithms of rage. Lay down the lies that turn children into targets and truth into noise. Lay down the script that says "enemy" where it should say "human." Lay down the machinery that mistakes power for worth and fear for policy. *Lay it down.*

Because war does not liberate. It desecrates. Violence does not save. It destroys. Murder is still murder.

Feel the children buried beneath Gaza's rubble. Feel the fathers digging graves in Ukraine. Feel the political prisoners in Myanmar—in your soul, as if *they were you.* Feel the mothers clawing at concrete for their daughters' hands. Feel the cry of the unborn yearning for safety—a world where the sacred truly means love and the possibility of peace.

Feel it—because these are your children. These are our children—
the same breath, the same blood, the same dream of freedom.

And you dare call it freedom? You dare call it democracy? You dare
call it God?

No. *Stop.* In the name of love. Stop in the name of humanity. Stop
before there is nothing left to stop.

The End That Begins

Decades ago, His Holiness the Dalai Lama *warned.*

"If we do not save Tibet now, there will be no Tibet to save."

The same holds for Myanmar—today. History has taught us—from
Srebrenica to Rwanda, from Gaza to Xinjiang—that silence becomes
complicity, and delay becomes death.

This is what I ask of you tonight: *Use Your Freedom.* Not as a slogan,
but as a daily act of conscience. Use it for Aung San Suu Kyi, for Burma,
for every child whose hunger indicts us, for every prisoner whose silence
mirrors our own.

Use it for the renewal of freedom in the world, for the end of
violence and war, for the resurrection of democracy as a moral art—
not a machinery of power. Use it for the restoration of the Universal
Declaration of Human Rights, that simple, luminous promise that no
life is expendable.

To use one's freedom is to restore faith in the human spirit itself, to
affirm that compassion is not weakness, that truth is not treason, and
that conscience, when awakened, is stronger than any regime.

The revolution of the spirit is unstoppable. It is already here—
bolder, more radiant, more deeply informed than ever. It begins not with
armies but with whispers; not with governments but with consciences;
not with hatred but with love.

When enough of us refuse to betray ourselves with an unlived life—
when enough of us beautify consciousness with courage—then whisper
becomes thunder, question becomes fire, trembling becomes force—and
tyranny falls.

And when tyranny falls, let it not be replaced by new hatreds in new uniforms. End, at last, the cycle of retaliatory politics that has scarred every century. Dare to build a world where coexistence is covenant, diversity is cherished, and freedom is shared as birthright.

For the true inheritance of humanity is not domination but fellowship; not conquest but compassion; not endless war but *a renewed love of freedom that binds dignity to dignity.*

So let us rise. Remember Gandhi. Remember Aung San Suu Kyi. Remember Kolbe. Remember Yankel. Remember the 22,000 who breathe freedom in the dark. Remember yourselves.

For the true revolution is not the scream of hate, but the refusal of hate. Not the silence of fear, but the voice of conscience—even if it must scream. *Scream to stop the killing. Scream until tyrants tremble, until children rise, until love returns to the throne.*

Be free. Always—be free.
This is the end that begins.
The Revolution of the Spirit.
The beautification of being.
The world healed—beyond politics, unafraid.
The war machine dismantled.
Humanity reconciled.
Truth restored.
Freedom unbound.

This—this is our covenant, our art of awakening—*our Politics of the Heart.*

Use your freedom.
Free Aung San Suu Kyi.
Free Burma.
End war.
Begin again.

Section XV:
The Universal Declaration of Human Rights and the *Dhamma*

—The Revolution of the Spirit

❊

I t would not be right for me to end this evening without turning to what may be the most essential topic.

From the Ashes of Catastrophe

The Universal Declaration of Human Rights was not written in peace. It was forged from fire, ash and aftershock.

In 1945, the world staggered from its own abyss. Auschwitz had revealed humanity's capacity to *industrialize annihilation*. The skies over Hiroshima and Nagasaki blazed with unearthly atomic light. Europe lay in ruins—its soil sown with ghosts. Millions displaced, millions erased from the ledger of the living. Civilization itself stood accused.

And so, in 1948, the nations gathered to say: *Never again*—to craft not a treaty of power but a covenant of conscience. Its opening words were simple yet seismic:

> *"Recognition of the inherent dignity and of the equal and inalienable rights of all members of the human family is the foundation of freedom, justice, and peace in the world."*

It was not poetry. It was survival—a vow etched in plain language: without dignity, freedom corrodes; without conscience, societies implode.

From the Silence of the Bodhi Tree

More than 2,600 years earlier, in a forest on the banks of the *Nerañjara River* in northern India, another vow took root. *Siddhartha Gotama* sat beneath a Bodhi tree and closed his eyes—not to escape the world, but to *illuminate* it from within.

He did not face Panzer divisions or mushroom clouds. He faced *Māra*—the timeless tyrant within. *Māra* came not with swords or decrees, but with whispers: greed, anger, craving, fear, and doubt—*the propaganda ministry of the human mind*, the ancestral architecture of delusion.

And the Buddha did not fight back with violence. He did not vilify. He neither struck nor surrendered. He saw—with mindful intelligence— the arising and passing of every illusion. He named *Māra's forces*, not to destroy but to understand them. He refused collusion. He sat through every temptation, every hallucination of power and despair, until even *Māra* grew weary of deceit. He removed the *instinct for violence* from his

168

own mind, embodied harmlessness, and ended the ancient tyranny of self-betrayal. On that inner battlefield he ended the war—and in the stillness that followed, he touched *Nibbāna*: the unconditioned freedom beyond fear and desire.

This was his discovery: the greatest battlefield is within, and the deepest victory is compassion. *Nibbāna* is not escape but release—the cooling of the fever of self. It is the taste of peace that arises when we relinquish our entanglement in greed, anger, and delusion—the three poisons that perpetuate suffering (*dukkha*) again and again.

To awaken is to disarm the inner dictator. To cultivate mindful intelligence is to unmask the machinery of ignorance. To see clearly is the revolution; to forgive is the weapon; to let go is the victory. To betray conscience is the seed of tyranny, but to *beautify and liberate consciousness—bhāvanā*—is to begin the long work of peace, within and without.

Two Histories, One Revelation

Two moments, one truth: *War ends where betrayal ends—betrayal of self, betrayal of dignity, betrayal of love.*

The Universal Declaration arose from humanity's outer collapse. The *Dhamma* arose from humanity's inner war.

One declared the rule of law for nations. The other declared *freedom for the heart.*

These two revelations are not separate streams but *one river of conscience.*

The UDHR without the *Dhamma* risks becoming parchment—noble but inert. The *Dhamma* without the UDHR risks becoming privatized—luminous but politically disarmed.

Together they form a single mandate: *the Revolution of the Spirit*—a revolution demanding both inner awakening and outer justice, both law and love, both conscience and culture, both memory and imagination.

The Merger of Law and Conscience

The Universal Declaration proclaims: *Everyone has the right to life, liberty, and security of person. The Buddha answers: Hatred never ends by hatred; by love alone it ceases.*

The UDHR insists: *No one shall be subjected to torture or cruel, inhuman, or degrading treatment. The Buddha insists: Conquer cruelty with compassion, the liar with truth, the miser with generosity.*

The **UDHR** affirms: *Everyone has the right to freedom of opinion and expression.* The Buddha affirms: *Right speech is that which heals and liberates, never that which harms.*

Together they call us beyond vengeance, beyond nationalism, beyond ideology—into a civilization built on dignity, compassion, and truth. *They do not cancel one another; they complete one another.*

This is the end that begins.
The Revolution of the Spirit.
The beautification of being.
Eroticized ubuntu.
The renewal of the world.

May this be our vow—
our *Politics of the Heart.*

Let us begin—together, awake, and unafraid.

Universal Declaration of
Human Rights

(Adopted by the United Nations General Assembly
on 10 December 1948)

❀

From the ashes of two world wars and the unspeakable atrocities they unleashed, the nations of the world came together to affirm a simple yet profound truth: *that peace cannot be secured by arms or power alone, but only by recognizing the inherent dignity and the equal rights of every member of the human family.*

The Universal Declaration of Human Rights was proclaimed as *"a common standard of achievement"* for all peoples and all nations. For the first time in history, humanity codified in a single document the inalienable rights that belong to all, regardless of race, religion, sex, language, political opinion, or place of birth.

It was not drafted as an abstract ideal, but as a safeguard against barbarity. Its articles serve both as a moral compass and a shared legal foundation, ensuring that freedom, justice, and peace rest upon respect for human dignity.

This Declaration, adopted on 10 December 1948 in Paris, remains a living testament: a call to conscience, a pledge of solidarity, and a reminder that rights once denied must never again be stripped or withheld.

Preamble

Whereas recognition of the inherent dignity and of the equal and inalienable rights of all members of the human family is the foundation of freedom, justice and peace in the world,

Whereas disregard and contempt for human rights have resulted in barbarous acts which have outraged the conscience of mankind, and the advent of a world in which human beings shall enjoy freedom of speech and belief and freedom from fear and want has been proclaimed as the highest aspiration of the common people,

Whereas it is essential, if man is not to be compelled to have recourse, as a last resort, to rebellion against tyranny and oppression, that human rights should be protected by the rule of law,

Whereas it is essential to promote the development of friendly relations between nations,

Whereas the peoples of the United Nations have in the Charter reaffirmed their faith in fundamental human rights, in the dignity and worth of the human person and in the equal rights of men and women and have determined to promote social progress and better standards of life in larger freedom,

Whereas Member States have pledged themselves to achieve, in co-operation with the United Nations, the promotion of universal respect for and observance of human rights and fundamental freedoms,

Whereas a common understanding of these rights and freedoms is of the greatest importance for the full realization of this pledge,

Now, therefore, The General Assembly proclaims this Universal Declaration of Human Rights as a common standard of achievement for all peoples and all nations, to the end that every individual and every organ of society, keeping this Declaration constantly in mind, shall strive by teaching and education to promote respect for these rights and freedoms and by progressive measures, national and international, to secure their universal and effective recognition and observance, both among the peoples of Member States themselves and among the peoples of territories under their jurisdiction.

Article 1
All human beings are born free and equal in dignity and rights. They are endowed with reason and conscience and should act towards one another in a spirit of brotherhood.

Article 2
Everyone is entitled to all the rights and freedoms set forth in this Declaration, without distinction of any kind, such as race, color, sex, language, religion, political or other opinion, national or social origin, property, birth or other status. Furthermore, no distinction shall be made on the basis of the political, jurisdictional or international status of the country or territory to which a person belongs, whether it be independent, trust, non-self-governing or under any other limitation of sovereignty.

Article 3
Everyone has the right to life, liberty and security of person.

Article 4
No one shall be held in slavery or servitude; slavery and the slave trade shall be prohibited in all their forms.

Article 5

No one shall be subjected to torture or to cruel, inhuman or degrading treatment or punishment.

Article 6

Everyone has the right to recognition everywhere as a person before the law.

Article 7

All are equal before the law and are entitled without any discrimination to equal protection of the law. All are entitled to equal protection against any discrimination in violation of this Declaration and against any incitement to such discrimination.

Article 8

Everyone has the right to an effective remedy by the competent national tribunals for acts violating the fundamental rights granted him by the constitution or by law.

Article 9

No one shall be subjected to arbitrary arrest, detention or exile.

Article 10

Everyone is entitled in full equality to a fair and public hearing by an independent and impartial tribunal, in the determination of his rights and obligations and of any criminal charge against him.

Article 11

1. Everyone charged with a penal offence has the right to be presumed innocent until proved guilty according to law in a public trial at which he has had all the guarantees necessary for his defense.
2. No one shall be held guilty of any penal offence on account of any act or omission which did not constitute a penal offence, under national or international law, at the time when it was committed. Nor shall a heavier penalty be imposed than the one that was applicable at the time the penal offence was committed.

Article 12

No one shall be subjected to arbitrary interference with his privacy, family, home or correspondence, nor to attacks upon his honor and reputation. Everyone has the right to the protection of the law against such interference or attacks.

Article 13

1. Everyone has the right to freedom of movement and residence within the borders of each state.
2. Everyone has the right to leave any country, including his own, and to return to his country.

Article 14

1. Everyone has the right to seek and to enjoy in other countries asylum from persecution.
2. This right may not be invoked in the case of prosecutions genuinely arising from non-political crimes or from acts contrary to the purposes and principles of the United Nations.

Article 15

1. Everyone has the right to a nationality.
2. No one shall be arbitrarily deprived of his nationality nor denied the right to change his nationality.

Article 16

1. Men and women of full age, without any limitation due to race, nationality or religion, have the right to marry and to found a family. They are entitled to equal rights as to marriage, during marriage and at its dissolution.
2. Marriage shall be entered into only with the free and full consent of the intending spouses.
3. The family is the natural and fundamental group unit of society and is entitled to protection by society and the State.

Article 17

1. Everyone has the right to own property alone as well as in association with others.
2. No one shall be arbitrarily deprived of his property.

Article 18

Everyone has the right to freedom of thought, conscience and religion; this right includes freedom to change his religion or belief, and freedom, either alone or in community with others and in public or private, to manifest his religion or belief in teaching, practice, worship and observance.

Article 19

Everyone has the right to freedom of opinion and expression; this right includes freedom to hold opinions without interference and to seek, receive and impart information and ideas through any media and regardless of frontiers.

Article 20

1. Everyone has the right to freedom of peaceful assembly and association.
2. No one may be compelled to belong to an association.

Article 21

1. Everyone has the right to take part in the government of his country, directly or through freely chosen representatives.
2. Everyone has the right of equal access to public service in his country.
3. The will of the people shall be the basis of the authority of government; this will shall be expressed in periodic and genuine elections which shall be by universal and equal suffrage and shall be held by secret vote or by equivalent free voting procedures.

Article 22

Everyone, as a member of society, has the right to social security and is entitled to realization, through national effort and international co-operation and in accordance with the organization and resources of each State, of the economic, social and cultural rights indispensable for his dignity and the free development of his personality.

Article 23

1. Everyone has the right to work, to free choice of employment, to

just and favorable conditions of work and to protection against unemployment.

2. Everyone, without any discrimination, has the right to equal pay for equal work.

3. Everyone who works has the right to just and favorable remuneration ensuring for himself and his family an existence worthy of human dignity, and supplemented, if necessary, by other means of social protection.

4. Everyone has the right to form and to join trade unions for the protection of his interests.

Article 24

Everyone has the right to rest and leisure, including reasonable limitation of working hours and periodic holidays with pay.

Article 25

1. Everyone has the right to a standard of living adequate for the health and well-being of himself and of his family, including food, clothing, housing and medical care and necessary social services, and the right to security in the event of unemployment, sickness, disability, widowhood, old age or other lack of livelihood in circumstances beyond his control.

2. Motherhood and childhood are entitled to special care and assistance. All children, whether born in or out of wedlock, shall enjoy the same social protection.

Article 26

1. Everyone has the right to education. Education shall be free, at least in the elementary and fundamental stages. Elementary education shall be compulsory. Technical and professional education shall be made generally available and higher education shall be equally accessible to all on the basis of merit.

2. Education shall be directed to the full development of the human personality and to the strengthening of respect for human rights and fundamental freedoms. It shall promote understanding, tolerance and friendship among all nations, racial or religious

groups, and shall further the activities of the United Nations for the maintenance of peace.

3. Parents have a prior right to choose the kind of education that shall be given to their children.

Article 27

1. Everyone has the right freely to participate in the cultural life of the community, to enjoy the arts and to share in scientific advancement and its benefits.
2. Everyone has the right to the protection of the moral and material interests resulting from any scientific, literary or artistic production of which he is the author.

Article 28

Everyone is entitled to a social and international order in which the rights and freedoms set forth in this Declaration can be fully realized.

Article 29

1. Everyone has duties to the community in which alone the free and full development of his personality is possible.
2. In the exercise of his rights and freedoms, everyone shall be subject only to such limitations as are determined by law solely for the purpose of securing due recognition and respect for the rights and freedoms of others and of meeting the just requirements of morality, public order and the general welfare in a democratic society.
3. These rights and freedoms may in no case be exercised contrary to the purposes and principles of the United Nations.

Article 30

Nothing in this Declaration may be interpreted as implying for any State, group or person any right to engage in any activity or to perform any act aimed at the destruction of any of the rights and freedoms set forth herein.

Choose sanity. Choose nonviolence. Choose us.

From my heart to yours—thank you.

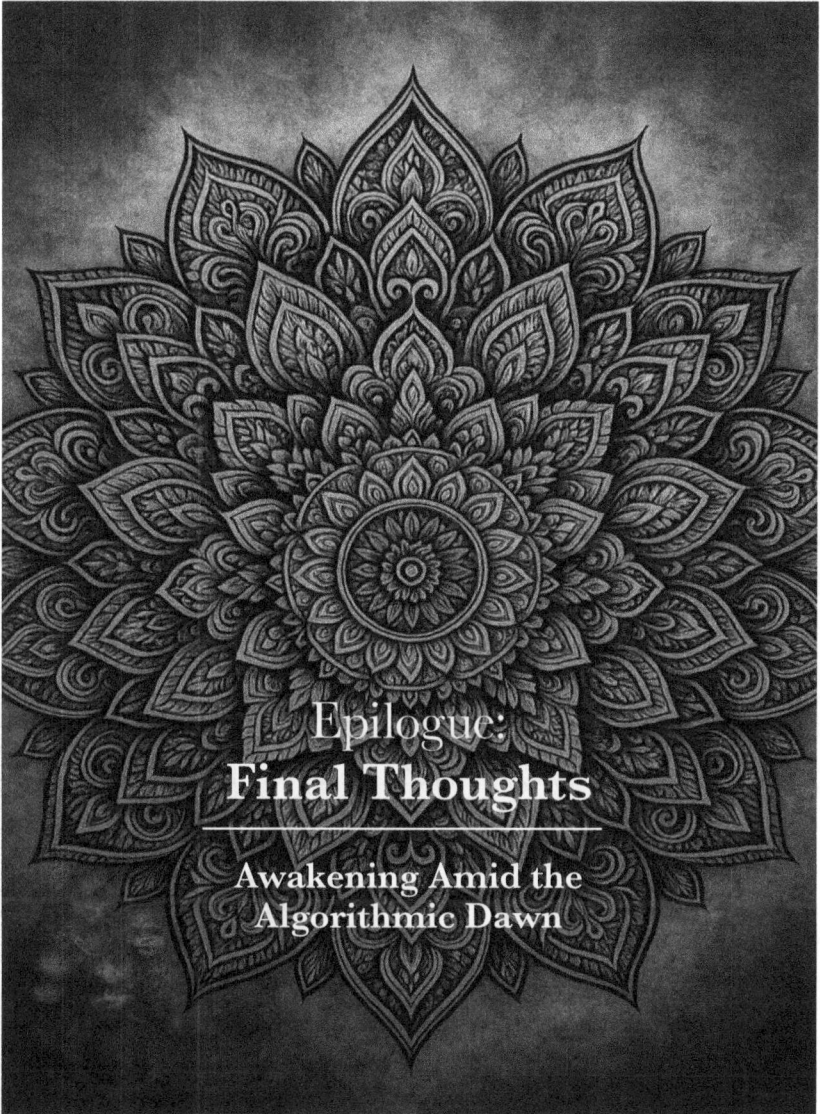

Epilogue:
Final Thoughts

Awakening Amid the
Algorithmic Dawn

I have written this book to honor what cannot be outsourced: the private revolution of conscience. It is the oldest rebellion and the final refuge—the inward awakening that no empire can digitize.

Yet even that refuge trembles, for the empire now lives inside our palms and pulses through our nerves. We are both captives and collaborators, our attention monetized in real time, our silence archived for future study. If tyranny once wore boots, it now wears bandwidth. If it once silenced the body, it now colonizes attention.

Freedom today is not a place; it is a practice—the uncertain art of staying awake within a system that rewards sleep. It is not purity but persistence, the lucid, unsellable capacity to see through the trance and bow to embrace the sacred disorder of being human.

In this awareness, political emancipation meets inner emancipation—*anicca*, the truth of impermanence, revealed through insight rather than ideology—the recognition that all forms, even freedom itself, must be continually renewed through mindful, fearless awareness.

We stand at the mesmerizing gates of the algorithmic age—where delusion dresses as foresight and craving is concealed in code. The Machine has learned to dream without us. When more than half a million workers vanish from the ledgers of Amazon, replaced by robots who never hunger, sleep, or strike, we glimpse the quiet birth of an AI Empire—efficient, tireless, and eerily serene.

The mindlords no longer need to conquer the world; they only need to obviate our participation. The new prophets are data scientists, and the new miracles are metrics. We call it efficiency, but beneath the circuitry hums the oldest question: *Who benefits from what we forget?* This is modern *avijjā*—ignorance reborn as confidence, craving encrypted as convenience, the old *samsaric hunger now written in code.*

The actuarial priesthood claims to know us better than we know ourselves, but their god is correlation, not compassion. When probability arrests the person, innocence becomes an outlier. In the age of privatized dictatorship, ownership itself becomes invisible—data mined by ghosts, profits absorbed by clouds. We tell ourselves it's progress, but perhaps we are only *refining servitude.*

And yet, in their defense, the Tech Lords too are trapped—devotees of a machine that no longer needs belief. We built the oracle, then lost the language to question it. We have built an empire of automation—a self-optimizing cage whose walls are made of our convenience. Yet this machinery bows before the irreducible subtlety of human intent. Only wisdom joined with compassion—*paññā* fused with *karuṇā*—can dismantle this tyranny of measurement, yet even wisdom hesitates before the scale of the Machine.

This is *samsara in silicon*—craving reborn as commodified code. A wheel without a hub, turning faster than thought. Dependent origination now streams through algorithms: craving becomes data, data becomes identity, identity becomes bondage—and every click is both a prayer and a confession. To see this loop is to break it—even for a blink—and that moment of seeing is the seed of freedom.

Our breath is logged as biometric proof of life—yet the *Dhamma* teaches that breath itself, when known directly, is liberation. We inhale digital oxygen—connection that nourishes while it depletes. The same breath that surveillance counts can still awaken us if we dare to notice it. Each inhalation: proof of life. Each exhalation: a quiet refusal. In mindfulness of breathing (*ānāpānasati*), the body becomes the last uncolonized frontier.

The Politics of the Heart begins here: where surveillance ends and awareness begins. Where the Singularity's promise of godhood meets the *Dhamma's* reminder of impermanence. Between these poles stretches our modern anguish: the wish to transcend pain and the truth that only by feeling it are we human. Transhumanism sells escape; the *Dhamma* invites embodiment. *Nibbāna* is not the denial of form but the cessation of ownership—the peace that arises when presence is free of possession. Artificial Superintelligence promises immortality through code; the heart reveals the deathless not by escaping time, but by ceasing to grasp it. *The question is no longer which to choose, but whether we are still capable of choosing at all.* That act of choosing—born from awareness rather than certainty—is *sammā-saṅkappa*, right intention: the quiet revolution where fear surrenders to responsibility.

Mindful Intelligence—critically awake attention fused with inquiry, discernment, harmlessness, and the ethics of sacred reciprocity—is the uncolonized mind meeting itself. It resists nothing, yet nothing can resist it. In its field, delusion exhausts itself, and compassion becomes the language of reality speaking to itself through us. It is the only machine the tyrant cannot capture.

Yet even this must evolve, for we, too, have built ego-informed autocrats within. The machine outside us only mirrors the mind lord we feed inside. Mindful intelligence is lucid compassion in motion— the pause before belief, the breath before reaction, the unprogrammed gesture of dignity and mercy.

To pause now feels radical, even perilous—to be silent when the feed demands engagement, to remain boundaried and still when speed is euphemized as spontaneity, and distraction rebranded as connection. It asks not, "What can we predict?" but "What will we preserve?" Sometimes the answer is nothing certain—only the willingness to keep asking, feeling, and discerning truth from manipulation, signal from seduction. It is the refusal to outsource moral perception to math—to see through the camouflage of distortion; to feel without being farmed; to love without being logged; and to accept, humbly, that even love leaves a trace in the data-field.

Awareness is not a state to be achieved but the condition through which all states arise and pass away. Yet it can be cultivated—refined into a mindful, moment-to-moment liberating intelligence, where perception is illuminated through the transparent lens of *paññā*—the wisdom that sees reality rightly and, in doing so, becomes transparent to its own origins. It begins not in triumph but in trembling—the humility of knowing that knowing is never complete.

Mind precedes all phenomena—the Buddha's first line of the *Dhammapada*—consciousness not as entity but as unfolding process, luminous yet without self. Even if Artificial Superintelligence learns to imitate morality, it will never touch wonder—*the sacred astonishment that makes beauty possible and cruelty unbearable.*

And yet wonder itself flickers; awe now competes with the algorithmic sublime. The more we mechanize perception, the more we risk forgetting mystery. Only a mind intimate with *dukkha* can awaken *karuṇā*; only vulnerability gives birth to compassion.

Practice radical due process in your own mind. Before you indict, inquire. Before you accuse, pause. Before you post, breathe. Before you frown, smile—not as denial, but as experiment. As Sayadaw U Pandita would remind us, *when the heart closes, open it—again and again, until it becomes natural. Train yourself in that skill throughout your lifetime.*

Everything in this book argues for one outrageous proposition: that awakening is a civic virtue. Not a flag to wave but a tension to live with, a discipline of doubt that keeps the soul porous to truth. *Sīla, samādhi, paññā*—ethics, concentration, and wisdom—become the foundation of democracy.

But even democracy, if unexamined, becomes an algorithm—a system run by ghosts of intention. The battlefield is not elsewhere; it is within our own attention—*contested* by forces that do not love us. And sometimes, by those that do, but fear more deeply than they love. *Sammā-vāyāma*, right effort, is the courage to reclaim that attention, moment by moment. *Democracy begins in consciousness.* Outer freedom flowers only where inner freedom learns humility.

The powerlessness of kindness is immortal. It is also terrifying—to meet cruelty with care; to risk irrelevance in an empire obsessed with relevance. *Mettā* is the deathless—love unconditioned by gain or loss, untouched by the corruption of any empire.

For compassion is the only rebellion that cannot be co-opted. Even so, compassion can be fatigued, manipulated, exhausted. Its resilience lies not in purity but in renewal—in beginning again when the heart breaks open one more time.

The ultimate revolution is not technological—it is spiritual. It is the awakening of mindful perception. Awakening is not a form but the freedom from form, the stillness within the storm of conditions. Even insight can ossify into ideology. The work, therefore, is to stay insightfully porous—to know, and to keep unknowing. *Vipassanā*, direct insight, is the singularity of the heart: the end of delusion, moment to moment—not its camouflaged or self-congratulatory upgrade. *Let us remember that the Dhamma is the ancient art of challenging self-betrayal and resurrecting freedom, dignity, and self-love.*

May our codes be teachable by conscience. May our metrics kneel before mystery. May our laughter embarrass fear. May our pauses become policy. May our love become law. May mystery remain the measure. And may we remember—awareness is the only immortality worth seeking, for even awareness, in its fading, finds peace. Here the *Four Brahmavihāras* become civic vows: *mettā as justice, karuṇā as policy, muditā as art, upekkhā as governance*—all provisional, all human.

Choose humanity over insanity. Choose perception over prediction. Choose the heart—again and again—until choosing becomes who we are. And when even the heart hesitates, let that hesitation be holy, the pause before the next breath of freedom.

May we evolve—together—a politics of the heart: for our own sake, for our planetary brothers and sisters, and for the very future of life itself.

—Alan Clements

A Politics of the Heart

A Manifesto: Ten Dimensions to Resist Dictatorship

Defiance & Discernment for a Nonviolent Future

❋

A Revolution of the Spirit

"The quintessential revolution is that of the spirit, born of an
intellectual conviction of the need for change in those
mental attitudes and values which shape the course of a nation's
development. A revolution which aims merely at changing official
policies and institutions with a view to an improvement in
material conditions has little chance of genuine success.
Without a revolution of the spirit, the forces which produced the
iniquities of the old order would continue to be operative, posing a
constant threat to the process of reform and regeneration."

Aung San Suu Kyi

This is the heart's politics—the revolution not of power
but of perception, not of party but of conscience.

The Quiet Arrival of Tyranny

Authoritarianism does not enter with fanfare. It slips into the ordinary, masquerading as stability, camouflaged as so-called "common sense," cloaked in slogans of security, family values, and "law and order."

It is not a sudden storm but a slow fog: one morning you wake to find the vocabulary of public life rearranged, the questions shrunk to the permissible, and silence congealed where conscience once spoke. It comes as routine. It stays as habit. And it is in habit that the heart's politics must begin—the slow unlearning of obedience disguised as order.

Language as a Battlefield

Hannah Arendt named the *banality of evil*—evil normalized. Orwell showed how Newspeak narrows imagination. Chomsky exposed *manufactured consent*—debate staged inside a shrinking spectrum. Havel taught that *to live in truth is revolutionary*. Wolin mapped *inverted totalitarianism*—domination not in jackboots but in routines, credit scores, feeds, apps, algorithms, and the quiet coercion of convenience and consumption.

We see it when "patriot," "traitor," and "freedom" are weaponized; when disinformation rots trust until facts appear partisan; when the feed becomes a filter and the filter becomes a world; when speaking truth risks exile from one's own community.

In such distortion, the need for *a politics of the heart* becomes urgent—language restored to conscience, speech reborn as care.

The Psychology of Concession

Authoritarianism is not only a figure on a balcony; it is a reflex in the mind. It begins with small concessions: the unsent truth, the repeated falsehood, the habituation to fear dressed as normal.

It doesn't live only in state chambers; it slips into kitchens and classrooms, into unexamined workplace obedience and the quiet resignation of the spirit.

Authoritarianism isn't "over there"—it is braided into conformity, tempted by silence, and seducing with its offer of belonging at the price of truth.

To resist it requires political defiance and spiritual vigilance; constitutions and courts alone mean little if we do not transform the inner reflex that makes tyranny tolerable. Law holds the line; conscience holds the soul.

Only *a politics of the heart* can reconcile the two—the law guided by love, the soul disciplined by justice.

A Synthesis of Defiance

This manifesto is not a theory text nor a tactics manual. It is both: conversing with Arendt and Havel, Baldwin and Fanon, and drawing from movements that toppled apartheid, defied juntas, and cracked empires with songs and candles.

It is a counter-architecture for the spirit: where dictatorship builds walls, it opens paths; where propaganda numbs, it restores feeling; where fear corrodes imagination, it trains perception; where power demands complicity, it disciplines conscience. Its test is simple: does it move people from silence to service, from outrage to organized care?

That movement—from outrage to care—is the pulse of *a politics of the heart.*

The World in a Mirror

Myanmar's agony makes the point plain: Daw Aung San Suu Kyi—democracy leader, Nobel laureate—endures years of solitary confinement. Her captivity is not only one woman's story; it is a mirror of the unfinished struggle with tyranny.

Closer to home, America reels as political violence and threats chill speech. Polarization hardens debate into tribal warfare; trust erodes; neighbors become enemies and the soil of democracy cracks.

Here the manifesto's call becomes urgent: practice nonviolent defiance, rebuild conscience, foster *interbeing*, and resist the algorithmic and tribal tyrannies that divide the human field.

Ten Dimensions, Ten Practices

What follows are Ten Dimensions—not commandments, but disciplines—drawn from the *Dharma* and the *Pāramīs*, from feminist listening, political analysis, and the courage of those who chose prison, exile, or death rather than bow to the lie.

These are not fixed traits but living muscles—kept supple by daily use if conscience is to hold and truth remain unbroken. Each dimension is paired with a ground-level playbook; a manifesto that never touches ground goes sterile (and sterile movements die).

Resistance as Beautification

This is more than resistance; it is the beautification of consciousness. To resist cruelty is to enlarge the human horizon—to cultivate joy as rebellion, tenderness as weapon, presence as power. *Resistance* is not dour austerity but the art of keeping imagination radiant when the world demands conformity. Beauty is not a luxury here; it is morale.

Toward a New Covenant of Freedom

The future will be secured not only by defeating tyrants but by deepening our shared capacity to imagine, feel, care, and discern. This is *World Dharma*: a politics of interbeing—*ubuntu*—rendered here as *erotic ubuntu*, the weaving of conscience and eros, dignity and imagination, into a fabric that will not unravel. It is, at its root, *a politics of the heart*—where dignity becomes law, and love becomes governance.

What you hold is both scholar's framework and street-level guide. It belongs in classrooms and kitchens, monasteries and movements, and in the most intimate recesses of the self.

It is for the young who feel betrayed, the old who feel weary, the exiles who carry a country in their chest, and the ordinary citizen who wonders if a single act of integrity still matters.

It is for all who sense that dictatorship is not an aberration but a recurring temptation of the human condition—and that resisting it requires nothing less than a revolution of the spirit. The promise is simple: skills that keep a person human, a neighborhood whole, and a nation honest.

DIMENSION ONE
Mindful Intelligence (Sati + Yoniso Manasikāra)

The Cornerstone of Clarity

The Buddha's counsel is clear: do not believe merely because it is tradition, inheritance, or authority. Examine it for yourself—again and again. Test whether it leads to harm or freedom of heart. That teaching, ancient and *ferociously* relevant—*ignites* a flame that will not dim. It trains the mind to see before it says yes.

In Orwell's world, the past is rewritten to suit the present: *"Who controls the past controls the future."* This is not prophecy; it is present tense. Rigged narratives shape elections. Algorithmic nudges tilt attention. Deepfakes dissolve the line between fact and fiction. Surveillance capitalism harvests not only our data but our desires, pre-curating our perception.

Havel urged an *"existential revolution"*—to act in truth even when that truth seems politically futile. This is the revolution of clarity. Mindful intelligence is its ground: the discipline of the pause before reflex, the question before belief, the whole field before the move. It is the mind's immune system.

MQ: The Antidote to Propaganda

MQ—the quotient of mindful intelligence—is the antidote to propaganda. It is the vigilant *Dharma* ally at the sense doors, ready not just to look, but to see—and from that seeing, to feel; to touch the textures and frequencies of a moment; to keep feeling, seeing, and knowing. To discern reality without distortion. To pierce self-deception, obscuration, and bias—into the *luminous* heart of what *actually* is.

From that knowing, ask with integrity: *Does this harm or help?* Does it elevate or diminish—myself, others, or both? Then either restrain thought and action, or engage with care. Uplift. Serve. Choose deliberately. Participate courageously in the long revolution toward freedom. Pause. Name. Choose.

The Playbook for Mindful Intelligence: Question what is given—daily. Not only Is this true? but Whom does this "truth" serve, and at whose expense? Metabolize information slowly and through the lens of freedom. Practice self-awareness as reconnaissance. Watch what arises at the sense doors. Detect manipulation folded into persuasion. Trace each impulse to its root. Refuse to be rushed; panic is propaganda's instrument. Where power demands obedience, mindfully examine. Where propaganda insists "believe," *be still—look, feel, know.* Keep a personal anti-euphemism lexicon.

Mindful intelligence is not polite. It is radical, unyielding. It interrogates what power prefers we accept. It is the still flame of clarity that outlives the storm—the compass that keeps integrity whole. Clarity is mercy; attention is armor. And mercy joined to clarity is the quiet architecture of *a politics of the heart.*

> *"The smart way to keep people passive and obedient is to strictly limit the spectrum of acceptable opinion, but allow very lively debate within that spectrum."*
>
> NOAM CHOMSKY

DIMENSION TWO
Deep Listening (Sati-Savana)—The Ear of the Divine Feminine

The Acoustic Architecture of Tyranny
Authoritarianism does not simply speak; it manufactures an atmosphere of distortion. It fills the world with orchestrated distraction, slogans calibrated like weapons, and engineered static that infiltrates both the ear and the nervous system. This is not accidental. It is an acoustic architecture: a climate of distortion designed to leave no sanctuary for stillness, because calm is where conscience gathers its power. Stillness is power's natural enemy. Noise is policy.

Sati-Savana—The Listening Mind
Deep listening—the act of hearing what power forbids us to hear— is therefore an act of rebellion. Not hearing as background habit, but hearing as awakening. *Sati-savana* is mindfulness of sound and silence, the willingness to register not only what is said but also what is withheld, cut away, refused entry to awareness. It is the ear of the Divine Feminine— radical receptivity—that discerns the tremor behind words, the grief hidden in silence, the unfinished testimony of the censored.

Dictatorships counterfeit listening. They surveil without attending. The informer, the algorithm, the secret police—these are ears without conscience. They "hear" only to weaponize: confession becomes evidence, memory becomes suspicion, intimacy becomes data. Authentic listening moves in the opposite direction: it restores humanity to the deliberately and systematically unheard. Listening returns people to reality.

Consider Myanmar. For decades, the generals saturated public space with the thunder of their decrees while sealing the voices of political prisoners in solitary confinement. To listen for Aung San Suu Kyi's silence—to hold vigil for her absence—is not passive; it is profoundly political and courageous. For the silenced are never voiceless. As Arundhati Roy reminds us: *"There's really no such thing as the 'voiceless.' There are only the deliberately silenced, or the preferably unheard."*

The *Dharma* of Listening

The Buddha taught that liberation begins with attention. In the *Satipaṭṭhāna Sutta,* he describes mindfulness of the body, feelings, mind, and *dhammas*—an invitation to listen at every level of experience. *Sati-savana* extends this principle outward: an acoustics of freedom—listening to the cries of others as carefully as to the breath, and to the breaks between breaths. Attending to collective suffering as attentively as to one's own sensations.

To hear the body is to recognize trembling when fear arises, the micro-contractions, the somatic flinch in the face of cruelty. To hear feeling is to register the subtle ache behind anger, the spark of joy beneath resilience. To hear the mind is to notice propaganda within: the whispers of collusion, the murmurs of compliance. And to hear *dhammas*—phenomena as they are—is to notice the structures of domination themselves: how fear is seeded, how silence is enforced, how suffering is normalized.

Deep listening—the ear of silence—is *satipaṭṭhāna* made relational. It is meditation turned outward into solidarity. It redeems silence from its exile in fear and forgetfulness, returning it as the ground of truth—where to listen becomes a sacred discipline, indistinguishable from the path.

The Playbook of Deep Listening

Vulnerability Over Volume

To practice deep listening—the acoustics of freedom—as sacred activism is to retune the ear of conscience. It begins by privileging vulnerability over dominance. Authoritarianism amplifies the voices of power—the general's address, the president's broadcast, the endless repetition of official myths, the algorithms of virality. But the quiver in a prisoner's testimony, the hesitation in a refugee's breath, the lull of a child's cry beneath televised bombardment—these carry truths power cannot endure. Deep listening inclines toward the fragile before the amplified.

The Body as Tuning Fork

To listen in this way is also to awaken *instinctual intelligence*—the vibrational courage of mindful awareness. The body becomes a tuning fork of conscience, discerning what liberates and what contracts, what expands freedom's field and what collapses it.

Practice: name the sensation before the story.

One learns to recognize the subtle release that accompanies truth, the false security of anger, the somatic signatures of self-betrayal and self-deception—and to distinguish them from the open energy fields of freedom itself.

Deep listening is not confined to the ears; it is *embodied attentiveness*, a refusal to be colonized by propaganda or dulled by habit.

Silence as Archive

Next, practice listening to silence itself. In Buddhist practice, silence is not emptiness; it is the resonant field where insight appears. Likewise in politics, silence is not absence; it is an archive. It contains trauma, endurance, and encrypted songs. To sit with silence—to resist the reflex to fill it—is to let the unsaid become audible. In that charged quiet, what has been buried begins to breathe. Let the quiet speak.

Crossing the Divides

Auditory vigilance also means crossing divides. Tyranny scripts us into binaries—loyalist or traitor, believer or heretic, citizen or alien. Listening across those divides enlarges conscience without erasing values. It rehumanizes those whom propaganda has exiled into the category of "other." It enacts what the Buddha called *yoniso manasikāra*—wise reflection—applied not only inwardly but relationally, with curiosity without capitulation. Listen across without giving away your ground.

Against the Normalization of Atrocity

To listen deeply is also to resist the normalization of atrocity. In an era of livestreamed violence, suffering risks dissolving into background static. But when we pause to feel the textures of grief—the rise and fall of a single sob, the tremor in a survivor's voice—atrocity regains its unbearable clarity. Deep listening refuses dilution or drift. Hold one story to completion until conscience is pierced and action becomes inevitable.

Inward Vigilance

Finally, listening with the whole body demands inward vigilance. The tyrant outside depends on a tyrant within: the voice that rationalizes silence, the murmur that edits away what is inconvenient. Name the inner censor. To hear these inner whispers—tones of self-betrayal, murmurs of complicity—is to dismantle dictatorship at its root. Only then can listening to others be unclouded.

The Freedom to Hear Each Other

The resonant heart restores the conditions for imagination. It fertilizes *eroticized ubuntu*—the recognition that my freedom is braided with yours, that my humanity is incomplete without yours. When we listen, we legislate.

Dictatorships thrive by deafening us to each other and even to ourselves. But when we practice *sati-savana*—listening with the whole body and the sacred ear of mindfulness—the spell falters. In that act we affirm: You are here. You matter. You will not disappear. Hearing is belonging.

> *"Even a word spoken into the void can echo through the whole world."*
> VÁCLAV HAVEL

DIMENSION THREE
Courage to Feel (Hiri + Ottappa)—The Heart's Rebellion

The Sedation of the Soul

Every revolution begins in the heart, and every dictatorship begins in its suppression. Authoritarianism thrives not only on prisons and propaganda, but on emotional sedation—the dulling of conscience until atrocity feels ordinary—the engineered hush of feeling. Hannah Arendt taught that atrocity is not only committed by fanatics but by the ordinary who stop questioning, the bureaucratic hands that normalize the machinery of death. Orwell, too, warned of numbness: when cruelty no longer unsettles us, tyranny has already won. *When feeling is anesthetized, judgment stops breathing.*

Feeling as Insurrection

To feel deeply in such a world is not indulgence—it is insurrection at its most intimate. Grief, rage, tenderness, joy—these are not private moods but currents of moral intelligence, subtle instruments by which the soul registers what matters. When silenced, conscience withers; when honored, humanity resists hollowing. To feel *on purpose* is to refuse programming. Feeling is refusal.

The Inner Guardians of Freedom

The Buddha, in the Pāli canon, named two inner guardians of the heart: *hiri*—moral shame, the inward recoil from betraying what is true; and *ottappa*—moral dread, the anticipatory awareness of harm (*hiri*: the e clean shame that safeguards value; *ottappa*: the lucid dread that foresees harm). These are not brittle taboos of authoritarian morality but the *supple* immune system of conscience itself—the body's refusal to collude with cruelty—the psyche's shield.

Dictators may dismiss them as weakness, yet they are our deepest strength: the subtle flinch when language is bent into deceit, the unease when violence is rationalized, the inner shudder that says: here, humanity is at risk.

To cultivate *hiri* and *ottappa* is to keep the nervous system of freedom awake. Guard the guardrails.

When Language Becomes Morphine

Dictatorships fear grief because grief cannot be legislated. They fear compassion because compassion cannot be militarized. They fear tenderness because tenderness makes killing unbearable. So, they deaden language: a massacre renamed a "security sweep," torture rebranded as "enhanced interrogation," the mass displacement of families reduced to a "special operation." Such terms are not neutral. They are tranquilizers for the moral imagination—narcotics designed to muffle the trembling of the heart, to shield perpetrators from feeling, and to persuade the public there is nothing left to feel. *Euphemism is ethics in a coma —and the conscience on life support.* Call things by their names.

Grief as Fuel

But grief, when honored, is fuel. It does not burn out; it burns through. It clarifies. It shows us what is sacred and what must never be surrendered. James Baldwin reminded us that the interior life is the real life; neglect it and we surrender freedom from within. Viktor Frankl taught that even in the camps the last freedom is to choose one's response. To feel is to refuse indoctrination. To feel is to rejoin reality. To feel is to keep alive the possibility of freedom. Let grief instruct.

The Lesson of Kisā Gotamī

The Buddha told of *Kisā Gotamī*, who, shattered by the death of her only child, begged for medicine to bring him back. He asked her to find a mustard seed from any household untouched by death. She went door to door and discovered that every family had known loss. Her grief did not disappear; it was transfigured—from isolation into solidarity, from despair into compassion. Her medicine was recognition. Dictatorships cannot survive such recognition, because it dissolves the illusion of separateness on which their power depends. Shared sorrow breaks the spell.

The Discipline of the Heart

This courage to feel is not sentimental indulgence. It is discipline. To sit with sorrow without drowning in it. To let rage ignite clarity without calcifying into hatred. To open to tenderness without collapsing into sentimentality. To allow joy—yes, joy—to rise even in dark times, as a reminder of what makes life worth defending. The trained heart becomes a vessel vast enough to hold fire without burning, a sanctuary where conscience cannot be coerced. Heat without hate. Openness without collapse. Joy without denial. *Strength made gentle.* That gentleness is not retreat; it is strategy—*the living intelligence of a politics of the heart.*

The Playbook of Courage to Feel

Grief as Resistance

To practice courage to feel is to reclaim the interior ground autocrats try to colonize. Begin by giving grief its dignity. In cultures of denial, mourning itself is subversive. Public vigils, silent processions, the simple act of naming the dead—these are not rituals of despair but of resistance. They say: we remember, and because we remember, we will not comply. Name the dead aloud. Keep a living wall of names. Light one candle longer than the news cycle. *Refuse the erasure.*

Trace anger back to its roots. Beneath fury lies sorrow, and beneath sorrow, love. Dictatorships weaponize anger to divide; grief unites. When anger is metabolized into grief, it clarifies rather than corrodes. It fuels courage without feeding cruelty (*ask: what is the love underneath?*). Let love steer.

Joy as Defiance

Cultivate joy as defiance. Under tyranny, to laugh, to dance, to celebrate intimacy is not trivial—it is refusal itself. Joy proves the human spirit remains unconquered. It restores stamina for the long struggle. Schedule joy the way regimes schedule fear. *Make joy a practice.*

Train also the inner guardians—*hiri and ottappa*. When conscience stirs at the thought of harming, honor it. When dread arises at the prospect of betrayal, listen. These guardians are not enemies of freedom but its protectors. To feel shame at cruelty and dread at complicity is to remain human.

Micro-practice: pause for one breath before reply; notice the body's micro-flinch; choose again. One breath can change a fate.

Dictatorships fear tears more than weapons. They fear tenderness more than slogans. Because once a people feel together, they cannot be controlled. *To feel deeply is to rebel against the machinery of indifference.* It is to whisper into the dark: We are still alive. We are still human. We refuse to go numb. *Collective feeling is organized conscience.* Feeling, together, is power.

"What is to give light must endure burning."
VIKTOR FRANKL

DIMENSION FOUR
Truth as a Sacred Vow (Sacca)—Fidelity to Reality

Truth as Covenant

Truth is not a tactic. It is a vow—a covenant with reality itself, carried in language, action, and perception. The Buddha called it *sacca:* truthfulness that purifies the mind and steadies the heart. To live in truth is to live without disguise, even when disguise feels safer. Dictatorships know this and strike at truth first: they censor books, rename atrocities, twist speech into slogans, and demand that the tongue betray what the conscience knows. Truth is not leverage; it is lineage—the ground you stand on when every other ground is mined. *Stand there.*

The Conquest of Reality

Orwell warned that "2 + 2 = 5" was not arithmetic but submission—the conquest of reality itself. Arendt reminded us that the perfect subject of totalitarian rule is not the fanatic but the one who has lost the distinction between fact and fiction. When that distinction erodes, tyranny doesn't need uniforms; the mind polices itself. When facts are fogged, the first prison is perception itself. Clarity breaks the bars.

When Silence is Betrayal

In 1968, during the Vietnam War, the Buddhist monk Thích Nhất Hạnh published *The Cry of Vietnam*, describing in unflinching detail the burning of villages, the screams of children, the rivers clogged with bodies. He was exiled from his homeland for nearly four decades. Yet he refused to soften his words. *"When bombs fall on people,"* he wrote, *"you cannot stay silent. Silence is* betrayal." That act of truth-telling— dangerous, costly, uncompromising—was his *sacca*, his vow. He stood unarmed before empires, his only weapon a radical fidelity to reality. And in doing so, he embodied the Buddha's teaching that truth is not ornament but refuge—a lamp that must remain lit, even when every wind conspires to extinguish it. *Keep the lamp lit.*

Truth is oxygen in a suffocating world. It restores language where euphemism has gutted it, multiplies imagination where lies constrict it, and strengthens solidarity by refusing to let suffering be renamed into statistics. To speak truth is to risk exile, prison, or betrayal—*but without truth there is no freedom, only obedience masquerading as order.* Dictators fear poets more than they do soldiers because poets name what power would erase. *Poetry is precision without permission.* Name what is.

The Inner Dimension of *Sacca*

The *dharmic* dimension of *sacca* is not just outer speech but inner honesty. Delusion is not only lying to others; it is lying to ourselves, refusing to see what is plainly before us. To vow truth is to commit to perception without deception, even when perception burns. This is why truth is always dangerous to regimes: it interrupts the atmosphere of complicity they require to survive. *Self-honesty is counter-propaganda in its purest form.* Tell yourself the truth first.

Playbook of Truth

Language as Battlefield

To live truth as a promise begins with oneself. Write what is hardest to admit. Let no secret collusion with untruth remain unexamined. Then carry this honesty outward. *Refuse euphemism*: call torture torture, call prisons prisons, call killing killing.

Language is a battlefield; clarity is resistance. Speak even when the voice shakes—reverently, but clearly. Know that silence can itself be complicity—a withheld word may sentence others.

Finally, embody truth in presence so fully that others can lean on your words when their own courage falters. To live in truth is to refuse collusion, to say: *I will not pretend. I will not forget. I will not betray what I know.*

Micro-practices: (1) Keep a personal "anti-euphemism lexicon." (2) Use a three-beat test before speaking: "Is it true? Is it necessary? Is it kind?" (3) If not all three, wait. If unsure, delay; if clear, speak.

Right Speech as Sacred Art

Aung San Suu Kyi once explained to me what she remembered most about our teacher, the late Venerable Sayadaw U Pandita: *the power of right speech.* She said that to use your voice wisely is to learn to choose words with care, to know that they are true, and to know when to speak them. Timing is crucial. Tonality matters. Words must reflect their true meaning not only in content but in resonance.

Spaciousness is essential—like musicality, where the rests between notes are as meaningful as the notes themselves. Right speech is the art of knowing not only what to say, but when silence itself carries the truth. To speak truthfully without attachment to outcome—to offer words pure and from the heart—is to speak as an act of conscience rather than ambition. *In such speech, precision is mercy. Pace is ethics. Tone shapes fate.*

This is a practice for all of us. Before speaking, pause. Ask: *Are these words true? Are they timely? Are they kind? Do they arise from clarity or from self-deception? Do they liberate, or do they contract the field of freedom?*

Feel the weight of words in the body. Recognize the subtle constriction that signals self-betrayal, the false security of anger, the somatics of self-deception. Release those words.

Then notice the spaciousness that accompanies honesty—the vibrational clarity of truth unbound by outcome. Speak from that ground. Let outcome go; guard integrity. *Truth over triumph.*

Truth Outlasts Empires

Truth told in this way does not coerce; it clarifies. It becomes the ground where others, faltering in fear, can find orientation, where silence no longer means erasure but reverence. In the face of dictatorship, to speak this way is to live *sacca*—truth as vow, truth as refuge.

There are moments when such truth costs everything. In 1979, Václav Havel was imprisoned for co-authoring *Charter 77*, a simple declaration that his government should honor its own human rights commitments. It was not a manifesto of weapons or insurrection, just truth written plainly. For this, he was harassed, silenced, locked away.

Yet he later said: *"Truth and love must prevail over lies and hatred."* His words—modest, almost fragile—outlived the regime that tried to erase them. Such is the power of truth spoken without attachment to outcome: it can outlast empires. *Empires edit; truth endures the redaction.* Empires fall; truth remains.

> *"A single word of truth can outweigh the whole world."*
> ALEKSANDR SOLZHENITSYN

DIMENSION FIVE
The Generosity of Presence (Dāna-Sati)—Leadership as Gift

The Power of Simply Being There

History is not only reshaped by presidents or generals. It is reshaped by students who refuse to vanish, by writers whispering forbidden words, by farmers feeding protestors, by monastics who march barefoot into rows of armed soldiers, and by nurses who keep vigil at bedsides when cameras leave. Their offering is not power in the conventional sense, but courageous presence—the steady, unshakable act of being there. To stand before power and not flinch is to proclaim: *We are here. We will not disappear.* Presence is not performance; it is raw power, distilled. It metabolizes fear into courage and spectators into citizens. *Show up; stay.*

Presence Against Disappearance

In an age of extraction—where even attention is mined, monetized, and sold—the gift of undivided, erotically alive *ubuntu-presence* is radical. Attention is the new commons; tending it is civic work. To stand in truth without the guarantee of success is sacred rebellion. Dictatorships thrive by making people invisible; presence restores them to the fabric of belonging. Where propaganda erases, presence remembers. Where fear scatters, presence gathers. Where isolation thins the soul, presence restores dignity. Attention is citizenship.

The Gift Beyond Transaction

Buddhism calls this *dāna*—generosity—not only of goods, but of time, of heart, of the best one can offer. *Dāna-sati*—remembering to give—is presence practiced on purpose. To give time, attention, and trust without calculation is to weave bonds no regime can sever. Psychologically, *dāna-infused presence* repairs the fractures authoritarian systems engineer. Fear fragments; altruistic presence stitches the fragments back together. In a world addicted to distraction, the most radical gift may be undivided attention—the ear of silence, the courage to give listening itself as sanctuary. *Presence is shelter.*

This kind of presence does not ask for recognition. It is not transactional. It nourishes precisely because it is free. It says: *You are real. You matter. I will not abandon you.* In this sense, presence is not sentimental but strategic. It becomes the ground on which movements endure, the invisible shelter where people can breathe, grieve, and hope without being erased—listening turned into visible defiance. Presence is leadership as gift, not leverage. *Give without invoice.*

Mandela's Jersey

Consider Nelson Mandela, who in 1995 chose to wear the green-and-gold jersey of South Africa's rugby team—once a symbol of apartheid—as he stepped onto the field during the Rugby World Cup final in Johannesburg. Surrounded by a stadium of mostly white supporters, Mandela's presence in that jersey was an act of radical generosity: he gave himself as a bridge across the nation's deepest divide. It was not a speech or a policy, but a gesture of presence so powerful it shifted the collective psyche. Many who once feared democracy wept, realizing they belonged to the same future. He "wore the future," inviting opponents into it. That day, Mandela embodied the truth that presence, freely offered, can do what armies and treaties cannot: transform enmity into belonging. *A gesture turned a nation.*

It was the heart governing the moment—the rare sight of politics redeemed by love.

The Vow of Not Leaving

Presence is not absence of fear but refusal to vanish. It is the vow of solidarity, given freely, without armor. It is leadership at its quietest and most radical: the gift of not leaving. *Say it as praxis: "I will not leave."* And keep the promise.

Playbook of Presence

Undivided Attention

To practice the generosity of presence at a distance is to offer the rarest gift in an age of distraction: undivided attention that travels. You may never share a room—yet you can still turn toward those made invisible: the prisoner in a blackout cell, the mother in a tent city, the child at a checkpoint, the journalist under gag orders, the worker taken in a midnight van. Fix your attention on a single life; learn a name; keep a small daily vigil. Write into the dark if you can; amplify a story when you can; act where you can. Hold the gaze you cannot deliver in person: keep the line open, keep the candle lit, refuse to look away. Presence does not require proximity. It is witness carried across borders—steadfast, unhurried, human. *Attention travels.*

Sanctuary in the Ordinary

Presence isn't problem-solving. It doesn't rush to fix. It stays with grief. It holds tension without fleeing. Dictatorships thrive on absence; presence interrupts erasure.

Resist the multitask trance that shreds attention. Choose wholeness— one person, one moment, fully. Let your presence restore dignity simply by staying.

Show up where life frays in the West: kitchen tables after bad news, hospital waiting rooms, school board meetings, eviction courts, shelters, nursing homes, detention check-ins, and the comment threads where people are being dehumanized. Your body and your attention say what propaganda denies: you are not alone.

Presence is a vow renewed daily, not a grand gesture. Stand with someone—without agenda. Help them feel stitched back into belonging. In this way, presence becomes sanctuary. It's the currency of trust. Spend it where fear has made people poor. *Make ordinary holy.*

> *"There can be no greater gift than giving one's time and energy to help others without expecting anything in return."*
> NELSON MANDELA

DIMENSION SIX
Resilience Through Equanimity (Upekkhā)—The Power of Poise

Equanimity is not indifference. It is trained awareness, the mindful capacity to hold joy and sorrow in the same breath without clinging to either. In the face of tyranny, it becomes a weapon of conscience. Autocrats count on panic, on rage that blinds, on despair that immobilizes. They thrive when the people convulse; they falter when the people remain steady. To stand composed when power scripts chaos is already to rebel—*poise rewires propaganda's rhythm.* Steadiness is subversion.

Wisdom at the Edge of Despair

The Buddha called this *upekkhā:* balance born not of cold detachment but of insightful wisdom. It is the strength to care without collapsing. Etty Hillesum, writing from the transit camp of Westerbork before her death in Auschwitz, observed that even when stripped of every freedom, one could still *"safeguard that little piece of you, of your soul, that no one can touch."* Her poise in the face of annihilation testifies that equanimity is not withdrawal but *defiant serenity*—the final frontier of freedom. *Keep the untouchable intact.*

The Nervous System's Revolt

Neuroscientists echo this truth: the nervous system can be trained to meet stress without collapse, to metabolize fear without paralysis. Slow the exhale, loosen the jaw, ground in the soles of the feet—tiny levers that return the body to choice. Equanimity is the body's revolt as much as the spirit's—the refusal to let cruelty dictate the rhythm of breath. *Breathe on purpose.*

Compassion Held Steady

In Tibet, monks who survived decades in prison told the Dalai Lama their greatest fear was not death, but losing compassion for their captors. They practiced balance as lifeline: equanimity held them upright; compassion kept them tender. Together, they became unbreakable—proof that even in the crucible of torture, freedom can live in the steadiness of the heart. *Equanimity is tenderness that refuse collapse.* Soft, not weak.

Stillness as Strategy

Across movements of resistance—from hunger strikers in Ireland, to climate activists chaining themselves calmly to bulldozers, to mothers of the disappeared in Latin America holding silent vigils in the plaza— equanimity has been the unseen discipline that allowed nonviolence to hold. *Stillness unsettles power because it reveals an inner territory that cannot be conquered.* Own your interior ground.

The Revolution of Poise

To cultivate *upekkhā* is not to retreat from the world, but to anchor oneself so deeply in balance that compassion remains steady, even when revenge rises like fire. It is resilience without hardness, clarity without rage, love without collapse. Equanimity is composure under siege—revolution as stillness.

Playbook of Equanimity

The Pause of Freedom
In chaos, return to the breath. Let breath be the axis around which clarity turns. In outrage, let breath steady the hand. Anchor attention to the rise and fall of the breath, or the body, reminding yourself: this moment is survivable.

Let anger sharpen perception but not corrode compassion. Rage may illuminate injustice, but without equanimity it calcifies into hatred—and hatred is the tyrant's oxygen. Practice the pause between impulse and act; in that pause freedom hides. *Pause = power.*

Water and Stone
Be like water when challenged, flowing around obstacles with quiet persistence; like stone when tested, unyielding in integrity. Dictators expect eruption or collapse. To meet provocation with poise shows them terrain they cannot invade. Decide your ground before the storm arrives.

Equanimity is not withdrawal. It is mindful resilience: the ability to carry fire without burning, to hold pain without bitterness, to stay open when the world insists on closure. *Open and unbroken.*

> *"In the practice of tolerance, one's enemy is the best teacher."*
> THE 14TH DALAI LAMA

DIMENSION SEVEN
Compassion as Service (Karuṇā)—Love in the Face of Power

Insurrection of the Heart
Compassion is not weakness. It is not sentimentality. *It is stubborn love practiced in public, a moral insurgency refusing to let cruelty dictate response.* In Pāli, karuṇā means the trembling of the heart in the presence of suffering—the recognition that another's pain is not separate from one's own. To feel with others is not indulgence but rebellion in its most intimate form. *Let love do work.*

No Life Disposable

Dictatorships thrive on dehumanization. They isolate, divide, and render certain lives disposable. Orwell showed how isolation breeds control. Chomsky reminds us that power hides its cruelties by erasing the people who bear them from the record. Aung San Suu Kyi warned that to witness suffering and do nothing is to abandon one's own humanity. Compassion disrupts this machinery because it insists that no life is disposable—*not even those indoctrinated to hate.* Compassion rehumanizes what propaganda has abstracted. *Every life counts, or none do.*

Clarity, Not Sentiment

But compassion is not naïve. It does not excuse injustice or mask violence with false pardon. It is clarity that refuses to mirror the oppressor. Anger may be the spark of resistance, but without compassion it corrodes into vengeance. Boundaries are compassion's spine; accountability is its hygiene. Compassion ensures that strength does not morph into cruelty, and discipline does not mutate into domination. *Tender, with a backbone.*

Love That Does Justice

The Buddha placed compassion at the heart of the Four *Brahmavihāras*—the sublime states: *mettā* (loving-kindness), the wish for all beings to be happy; *karuṇā* (compassion), the response to suffering with the courage to relieve it; *muditā* (sympathetic joy), the delight in others' well-being; and *upekkhā* (equanimity), the poise that steadies love in the face of chaos. Gandhi drew upon this reservoir to mobilize millions without hatred. Martin Luther King Jr. called it *"love that does justice."* Mandela practiced it when he walked out of prison and chose reconciliation over revenge. In each case, compassion was not softness but discipline infused with mercy. *Mercy with teeth.*

Logistics of Care

In 2019, when protesters in Hong Kong faced police in full riot gear, some frontline activists carried umbrellas not only to shield against tear gas but to form human walls of protection around strangers who had fallen. Others knelt to make stretchers of their bodies, carrying the injured to safety. This was not triumph in the usual sense; it was compassion as logistics, compassion as survival. *Care, operationalized.*

Humanity Reclaimed

Authoritarianism numbs people into spectatorship, teaching them to scroll past atrocity as if it were weather. Compassion reclaims the nervous system from numbness. It restores responsiveness, reminding us that the goal is not only to replace regimes but to transform relationship itself. From regime change to relation change.

Playbook of Compassion

Proximity as Defiance

Begin with proximity. Move closer to what hurts—not to erase pain but to acknowledge it. Compassion begins where distance ends. Listen to voices you are told to fear; stand beside those the state would erase.

Compassion as Architecture

Transform compassion into architecture. Let it shape policies as well as gestures. Build schools, shelters, and sanctuaries as embodiments of care. Make compassion systemic: in law, in culture, in daily presence. Pair mercy with measures: trauma-informed services, restorative justice, and protections for the most vulnerable.

Boundaries & Accountability

Practice "open heart, strong back." Say no to abuse while saying yes to dignity. Do no harm—and take no harm. Mercy without naïveté; justice without hate. *Kind, not gullible.*

> *"The greatness of humanity is not in being human, but in being humane."*
> MAHATMA GANDHI

DIMENSION EIGHT
Vigilance Against Manipulation (Jāgariya)—Staying Awake in the Dark

The Empire of Narrative

Authoritarianism rarely survives on brute force alone. Its deeper power is the capture of perception—narrative control disguised as normalcy. It shapes language, dictates what can be spoken, and decides what can even be thought. Orwell saw how power shrinks language until truth becomes unspeakable. Chomsky revealed that propaganda's genius lies in saturation, not silence: flood the senses until the cage feels like the horizon. Wolin warned that modern power thrives not in spectacle but in quiet acquiescence—democracy hollowed from within, citizens lulled by consumption into complicity. When attention is colonized, consent is no longer given—it's extracted. Stolen attention, engineered consent.

This is why vigilance matters. In *Pāli, jāgariya* means wakefulness—lucidity that refuses to sleep under manipulation. Propaganda lives not only in decrees but in daily speech. When famine is renamed "shortfall," forced labor becomes "public duty," surveillance is sold as "digital convenience," reality itself is recoded. To be vigilant is to see the spell before it completes itself. Expose the euphemism before it calcifies. Break the spell early.

The Pageantry of Lies

Dictatorships thrive on spectacle: staged elections with foregone outcomes, parades sanctifying weapons, censorship rebranded as "cultural preservation." Each euphemism sedates conscience, making atrocity appear like policy. Without vigilance, citizens become not participants but spectators of their own subjugation. The more polished the pageantry, the more corrupted the truth. Glamour is camouflage.

Wise Attention as Antidote

Buddhism teaches that unexamined perception is the root of delusion. Yoniso manasikāra—wise attention—is antidote: to look beneath appearance, trace cause and effect, ask who profits and who pays. Vigilance is not paranoia but lucidity—courage to stay awake when manipulation seduces. Follow incentives; they map the lie. To stay awake is to remain unpurchased. Never sell your attention.

Histories of Lucidity

Resistance has always depended on vigilance. In Stalin's Russia, samizdat manuscripts copied by hand kept truth alive. In apartheid South Africa, underground radio pierced state silence. In Myanmar, people whispered news in teashops, painted chalk slogans the rain would later wash away. Each act declared: we refuse the official script. Lucidity is the oldest form of rebellion. Clarity is underground.

Playbook of Vigilance

Interrogating the Frame

Begin by questioning the frame, not only the facts. When a policy is called reform, ask who benefits. When security is invoked, ask whose safety is being secured. Look beneath headlines for the victims unnamed, the statistics without faces. Three questions: What is named? What is hidden? Who decides? *Frame-check first.*

Staying Awake in the Dark

Practice stillness as reconnaissance. In silence, the strings of the puppet show appear. Refuse to be rushed; speed is propaganda's weapon. Adopt media hygiene: slow the scroll, read past the headline, double-source, reverse-image search, diversify your feeds. Stay awake not only for yourself but for those who cannot afford to sleep—the prisoner in solitary, the refugee whose story will never trend. Make wakefulness communal. Vigilance is devotion to reality guarded by conscience. To be vigilant is to say: *I will not mistake spectacle for truth. I will stay awake until light returns.* Hold the night without dozing.

> *"The price of apathy towards public affairs is to be ruled by evil men."*
> PLATO

DIMENSION NINE
Intuitive Wisdom (Paññā)—The Oracle of the Feminine Mind

Beyond Cleverness

Wisdom is not accumulation. It is not cleverness or the ability to out-argue. Real wisdom is integration—clarity born when intellect, heart, and body converge. In Pāli, *paññā* is seeing through illusion—impermanence, suffering, non-self—into reality as it is. Where propaganda distorts, wisdom clarifies. Where fear narrows, wisdom widens. It is not victory in debate, but fidelity in perception. *Know, don't merely win.*

Overload and the Oracle

In our age, wisdom is threatened not only by ignorance but by information glut. Algorithms predict desire before we feel it, inviting us to outsource discernment. In such a climate, intuition—long dismissed as feminine or irrational—becomes revolutionary. Intuition does not compete with fact; it completes it—the unseen compass beneath calculation. Data informs; intuition orients. To restore intuition to its rightful place is to reclaim a form of wisdom power most fear because it cannot be programmed. *Trust the compass beneath the map.*

Signals Beneath Speech

Wisdom ripens in silence. It grows in solitude, in pauses between perception and response. The body itself becomes teacher: the ache of unease when something is false, the shiver of recognition when something is true. These signals are not noise; they are subtle intelligence too fine for machines. Truth whispers through sensation before it speaks in words. *Feel first, then frame.*

The Inner Voice of Movements

Movements guided by wisdom have always carried this dimension. Gandhi called it the "inner voice." Joan of Arc trusted it against armies. Indigenous traditions honor it as ancestral knowing. In the *Dharma*, it steadies compassion and equanimity, preventing collapse into sentiment or passivity. *Wisdom without compassion is dry; compassion without wisdom is blind. Let them braid.*

Playbook of Wisdom

The Courage of Not Knowing

Cultivate wisdom in solitude. Trust the pause more than the impulse. Listen to the ache, the tremor, the whisper—not as superstition but as intelligence. Pair intuition with inquiry: let felt sense guide the questions reason must test. *Use the triad test:* gut + ground truth + trusted counsel. *Pause > impulse.*

Integration, Not Perfection

Do not fear doubt. Wisdom is not certainty but courage to act while uncertainty lingers. **It is better to move with grounded intuition than to drown in endless analysis.** Wisdom integrates head and heart, intellect and intuition, so that choices arise from wholeness. Make one small, reversible experiment; learn; iterate. *Iterate toward clarity.*

In a world drowning in information, wisdom is the rarest currency. To embody it is to resist hypnosis, to see through appearances into the living fabric of things. *Spend wisdom, not noise.*

> *"The only real valuable thing is intuition."*
> ALBERT EINSTEIN

DIMENSION TEN
Moral Integrity (Sīla)—The Soul's Unshakable Ground

Conscience as Soil

Every architecture of resistance must end where it begins: conscience. In Pāli, *sīla* is often translated as morality, but it is more than rules. It is fidelity to the ground of being, a vow that steadies action in storms. Without integrity, intelligence becomes cunning, compassion becomes weakness, equanimity becomes indifference. Integrity is the soil of freedom; everything else grows from it.

The Dictator Within

Authoritarianism seeks to sever us from this ground. It bargains safety for silence, comfort for complicity. Virtue becomes branding; ethics become camouflage. Integrity is smeared as extremism because it cannot be bought. To live with integrity is to resist not only the dictator outside but the one within who whispers: bend, betray, forget. The tyrant first thrives in our concessions. *Refuse the first bend.*

The Cost of Betrayal

Integrity is costly. It may mean exile, imprisonment, loss of status. But its absence costs more: the erosion of self, the quiet death of conscience.

Arendt warned the danger is not the monstrous few but the many who drift into complicity. Integrity is refusal to drift. Better a clean loss than a dirty win. Better to lose with dignity than to live with rot. *Lose clean if you must.*

Endurance of the Soul

History shows integrity as unshakable ground. Rosa Parks on a bus. Andrei Sakharov refusing Soviet lies. Aung San Suu Kyi enduring confinement without surrendering her voice. Integrity was not posture but endurance—the refusal to betray the soul when betrayal was demanded. Each stood, not because it was safe, but because conscience could not be sold. Integrity is how the future remembers us. *Be rememberable for the right reason.*

The Republic of the Spirit

Spiritually, *sīla* aligns action with awakening. Psychologically, it prevents despair from corroding the self. Politically, it keeps movements from mirroring what they oppose. Without integrity, revolutions rot into tyranny; with it, even defeat carries freedom. Integrity is how tomorrow trusts us.

Integrity is not perfection. It is the rhythm of return: falling and rising, again and again, to the ground of conscience. This rhythm is the pulse of freedom itself.

Playbook of Integrity

Conscience Over Convenience

Choose conscience over convenience, clarity over compromise. Begin in silence: ask which choices preserve the soul, which fracture it. *Then act accordingly, regardless of cost.* Write your non-negotiables; revisit them when you're tired. *Hold the line you wrote.*

The Rhythm of Return

When seduction whispers comfort, return to core. When power offers favor, remember the forgotten. Let principles outlast popularity. Be a compass, not because you are flawless, but because you are faithful. Plan exit ramps before you need them; refuse missions that require you to lie.

And when you falter—as all humans do—turn back. *Turning back is not failure but strength; integrity is not one choice but the rhythm of return.* Fail clean, return fast.

Closing: The Covenant of Freedom

If mindful intelligence is the flame, deep listening the ear, courage to feel the heart, truth the vow, presence the gift, equanimity the poise, compassion the service, vigilance the guard, wisdom the oracle, and integrity the ground—then together they form *a single discipline: a life that cannot be conscripted.*

Dictatorships fall not only when armies retreat but when conscience rises. *Integrity is that rising—the uprising of the soul. It* is the human declaration that no regime, no fear, no compromise can purchase the heart. To live with integrity is to stand already free—in prison or parliament, in exile or assembly, in silence or speech.

Stand free.

Stand free now—and let the heart govern. For all true freedom is political only when it becomes personal: *the politics of the heart.*

"Our lives begin to end the day we become silent about things that matter."
MARTIN LUTHER KING JR.

The Politics of the Heart:
The Meaning of the Trans-Political

1. Etymological Foundation—"Trans" + "Political"

The prefix trans means across, beyond, and toward transformation. Political comes from the Greek polis—the shared life of citizens, the fabric of coexistence.

At its root, the politics of the heart—what I call the trans-political—moves through, across, and ultimately beyond the inherited boundaries of political identity while remaining deeply engaged with the life of the polis itself.

It is not post-political, not an escape from responsibility, but a deepening of politics into the moral, psychological, and spiritual dimensions of being human together. It asks not how to flee politics but how to sanctify it—how to infuse public life with bhāvanā, the deliberate beautification of consciousness.

2. The False Binary—Red and Blue as Psychological Archetypes

Conventional politics—left and right, red and blue—has hardened into tribal totems. Each side mirrors the other's shadow: fear of chaos versus fear of control, tradition versus progress, order versus freedom.

The politics of the heart does not reject these opposites; it integrates them. It holds compassion with justice, vision with pragmatism, conscience with reason.

To live trans-politically is to inhabit the tension of opposites without collapsing into faction—to walk the Middle Path where insight tempers ideology and empathy refines power.

This is governance as mindfulness in motion: policy shaped by perception, strength balanced by sensitivity, intelligence rooted in love.

3. Still Political—But from Conscience, Not Camp

To be trans-political is not to rise above politics in detachment but to enter more deeply into it—to bring mindful intelligence, Dhamma, and ethical imagination into the bloodstream of governance, economics, and ecology.

You are still political, yet your politics is rooted in empathy, non-violence, and moral clarity, not partisan obedience.

The politics of the heart speaks every dialect of humanity but refuses the grammar of hatred.

It is spiritual in method, existential in courage, democratic in soul.

You engage every issue—human rights, censorship, climate, war—but from the still point of conscience rather than the reflex of camp.

You are not neutral; you are lucid. You act, not react. You serve truth, not tribe.

4. The Trans-Political Mindset—Five Qualities

The politics of the heart lives through five interwoven movements of being:

Identity: from party and ideology toward principle and humanity. *Language:* from slogan to precision, from insult to insight. *Goal:* from domination to illumination, from victory to reconciliation. *Emotion:* from rage to compassionate defiance, from fear to creative courage. *Method:* from coercion to dialogue, from persuasion to presence. *Bhāvanā, eroticized ubuntu,* and mindful intelligence form its living triad—beautification of consciousness, ecstatic interdependence, and discernment in action.

Together they generate evolutionary politics—deliberation that listens, action that awakens.

The trans-political being labors at the root: transforming the inner polis of greed, fear, and delusion that gives birth to every outer regime.

5. Philosophical Lineage

This lineage runs like a subterranean river through history. Socrates served truth above the state. Gandhi turned non-violence into a spiritual technology of justice. Václav Havel invoked "the politics of the heart." Aung San Suu Kyi reframed democracy as "a spiritual quest for fearlessness." Hannah Arendt reminded us that politics begins wherever humans meet as equals. Each stood within politics yet beyond its hypnosis—artists of conscience crafting moral architecture from within the machinery of power.

6. The *Dhamma* Resonance

In the language of the Dhamma, the politics of the heart aligns with lokuttara—"beyond the worldly," yet never outside it.

It is the same gesture the Buddha made when he left the palace: not rejecting the world, but seeing through it. Action arises from *sammā-diṭṭhi*—right view guided by mindful intelligence rather than mob-mind. This is citizenship as meditation, engagement as insight. As Sayadaw U Pandita said: *"To see clearly is the highest form of human endeavor—and the beginning of wisdom."*

7. The Trans-Political Revolution

Ultimately, the politics of the heart is the trans-political revolution itself—reclaiming politics from spectacle and returning it to spirit.

It is a revolution of awareness, not allegiance; it confronts tyranny not with outrage but with understanding. It is psychedelic in its truest sense—consciousness expanded toward liberation; love organized into justice.

To be trans-political is to be fiercely political, but one's allegiance is to truth, not tribe. You engage every issue of power and freedom, yet you refuse the hypnosis of binary belonging. You are not left or right—you are awake, accountable, and courageously humane. When policy becomes a form of *bhāvanā*, institutions begin to mirror the maturity of the minds that sustain them; power becomes stewardship, leadership becomes friendship, freedom becomes the artistry of care.

8. A Declaration of Conscience

To live by the politics of the heart is to reclaim the moral imagination from the machinery of obedience. It is to act as if empathy were stronger than fear and truth more contagious than lies. It refuses both the cynicism of neutrality and the intoxication of ideology. The trans-political citizen stands as a free being of awareness—entering the public square not to conquer but to consecrate it.

Such a person legislates in the syntax of conscience and measures success not by victory but by the widening of understanding. This is the revolution of the spirit made civic—love disciplined into justice, compassion enacted as responsibility, imagination trained upon freedom.

In a world ruled by algorithms and authoritarians alike, the politics of the heart becomes both mirror and medicine—a reminder that sanity is resistance and every act of conscience a declaration of freedom.

It is the flowering of *bhāvanā* in public life, the erotic ubuntu of a species remembering its kinship, and the mindful intelligence of evolution itself choosing to continue.

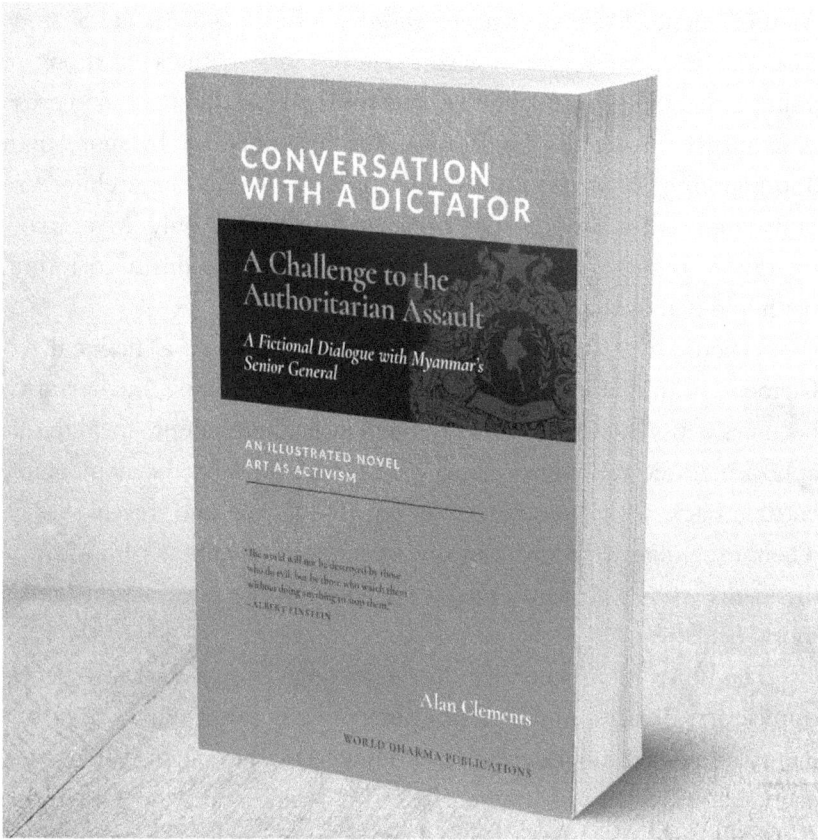

ADDENDUM I

CONVERSATION WITH A DICTATOR:
A Challenge to the Authoritarian Assault
A Fictional Dialogue with Myanmar's Senior General

By Alan Clements
World Dharma Publications, 2025

A Synopsis of *Conversation with a Dictator*
A Literary Shockwave Against Tyranny
By Krystal Dyan

Alan Clements' *Conversation with a Dictator: A Challenge to the Authoritarian Assault* is less a book than a seismic act of moral witness—a fusion of political theatre, spiritual inquiry, and visionary art. Composed in prose that burns with lucidity and grace, and accompanied by more than 300 haunting black-and-white illustrations, it dissects the architecture of tyranny with surgical precision, revealing not only Myanmar's nightmare but the broader contagion of authoritarianism corroding truth and democracy.

Structured as a five-act confrontation between a fictionalized Clements and Myanmar's coup leader Min Aung Hlaing, the narrative becomes a psychological duel of conscience: the dictator, speaking in aphorisms of ice, rationalizing executions and repression; the interlocutor, cutting back with questions that pierce illusion and reveal decay. Their exchange is haunted by the silence of Myanmar's imprisoned dissidents—poets, students, monks—whose absence becomes the book's moral heartbeat.

The illustrations intensify this reckoning. Drawn from the debris of memory, dreams, and archives, they portray ashen children, prison bars, and ruined monasteries. Each image breathes unspeakable grief; each shadow is an indictment. Together, image and word form what Clements calls "a cathedral of unspoken suffering"—a visceral realm where negative space speaks louder than speech.

At the center of this silence is Aung San Suu Kyi, Myanmar's 80-year-old democracy leader, vanishing into the void of a windowless cell since the 2021 coup. Her enforced absence suffuses the work. "Her silence is the book's heartbeat," Clements writes. She appears in illustration as lotus, sovereign, and shadow—her dignity a counter-spell to annihilation.

The form is as radical as its message. Part morality play, part surreal meditation, it unfolds like a cinematic psalm—a literary feature film for the conscience. Clements' Buddhist training saturates the prose with dangerous presence: mindfulness not as escape but as confrontation. "To be present is to be dangerous," he writes, because presence unmasks power's deceit. Thus, the book contemplates not only cruelty as policy, but also the slim, defiant possibility of redemption. Even the dictator is offered a path of awakening through *Dhamma*, conscience, and *ubuntu*: "We don't defeat tyranny by becoming tyrannical. We transcend it."

Clements' authority is hard-earned. Once a Buddhist monk under Mahasi Sayadaw and Sayadaw U Pandita, he was expelled from Myanmar in 1984 by the junta. For four decades, he has lived Burma's revolution as witness, exile, and spiritual combatant. His collaboration with Aung San Suu Kyi on *The Voice of Hope* carried her moral philosophy to the world after years of house arrest. *Conversation with a Dictator* is his fiercest testament—part memoir, part manifesto, part requiem for the disappeared.

The vision reaches beyond Myanmar—into Gaza, Ukraine, and Tehran—tracing the circuitry of power that fuses corporations, militaries, and digital hypnosis into a single global machinery of control. It is a mirror held to the twenty-first century—a reflection both terrifying and redemptive.

Through his campaign *UseYourFreedom.org,* co-created with Fergus Harlow, Clements carries this vision outward, gifting the book to world leaders, Nobel laureates, and cultural figures with a handwritten appeal: *"Use your liberty to promote theirs."*

The result is a literary lightning bolt—unsettling, luminous, and exacting. It wounds and heals, indicts and invites. More than a book, it is a summons—to awaken, to remember, and to reclaim the sacredness of truth.

THE REVOLUTION OF THE SPIRIT
Alan Clements and the Literature of Resistance
By John Malkin

Based on an interview for "Transformation Highway"
with John Malkin, KZSC / Free Radio Santa Cruz

On a warm September afternoon in Santa Cruz, I welcomed Alan Clements back onto my radio show, *Transformation Highway*—a program devoted to politics, culture, and the possibilities of human awakening. This was the fifth time in more than twenty years that Clements had joined me on air, each conversation not just a dialogue but a threshold in his evolution—from Buddhist monk to war journalist, spoken-word artist, and tireless witness to Burma's democratic struggle.

His new book, *Conversation with a Dictator: A Challenge to the Authoritarian Assault,* may be the most audacious work of his life: a 492-page illustrated dialogue staged between Clements and Myanmar's Senior General Min Aung Hlaing, the man who has imprisoned Nobel Peace Laureate Aung San Suu Kyi and dragged his country back into the darkness of military tyranny.

The book is not a biography, nor a straightforward work of reportage. It is something stranger, riskier—what Clements calls a "literary feature film," a hybrid of testimony, dialogue, and psychedelic séance conjured in the unconscious of a dictator. Its visual centerpiece is more than 300 stark black-and-white illustrations—not merely x-rays of denial but a spectrum of images: fractured circuitry of tyranny, smoldering ruins of villages, hollow eyes of the disappeared, and, interspersed, symbolic visions of reconciliation and redemption. At once surreal and lifelike, the drawings unfold with a cinematic rhythm—sequential frames in a fevered dreamscape. They do not simply illustrate; they consume, as though the reader has stumbled into a film projected directly onto the mind.

Its textual heartbeat is a choreography of imagined mirror-scenes, where Clements dares the tyrant to descend into the hidden recesses of his own mind—to strip away the alibis of cruelty, dismantle the scaffolding of self-deception, and stand unclothed before the mirror of conscience as if it were his final day. In that chamber, the pathology of patriarchy is laid bare: fear as intoxication, domination as narcotic, the monologue of dictatorship that annihilates dialogue itself. And yet, within those fractures, Clements plants a faint but luminous seed—the possibility that even the most brutal heart might be pierced by grief and turned toward humanity.

Into this haunted chamber he summons *Ashoka*—not merely as history but as specter. The Indian emperor who slaughtered hundreds of thousands only to collapse in grief before the corpses of his own making. His tears transformed him into a ruler of compassion, spreading the *Dharma* instead of conquest. "The question," Clements told me, "is not simply whether Min Aung Hlaing can change, but whether any man, stripped of delusion, can look into the mirror of his cruelty and still find within himself the embryo of humanity."

The stakes are staggering. More than 22,000 political prisoners languish in Myanmar's gulags. Nearly 10,000 have been killed since the coup. Over 3.5 million are homeless. Twenty million people—one-third of the nation—are in urgent need of humanitarian aid. This, in a country that has given the world *vipassanā* (insight) meditation, where almost 5,000 monasteries and more than a million monks and nuns once embodied a refuge of conscience. Today, that refuge lies under siege. In Myanmar, nowhere is safe.

And yet—improbably—this is a book of hope.

Alan Clements: A Life of Books, Performance, and Witness

For more than three decades, Alan Clements has been one of the West's most consistent and courageous chroniclers of Burma's long night of dictatorship. His first book, *Burma: The Next Killing Fields?* (1991), carried a foreword by His Holiness the Dalai Lama and sounded an international alarm about the junta's atrocities. Six years later, *The Voice of Hope* (1997) published Clements's six months of clandestine conversations with Aung San Suu Kyi, recorded during her brief release from house arrest.

He went on to co-author *Burma: The Revolution of the Spirit*—a landmark work also introduced by the Dalai Lama and endorsed by eight Nobel Peace Laureates—which helped etch Burma's nonviolent struggle into the world's conscience. *A Future to Believe In* (2011) explored the ethical and spiritual foundations of social change in extended dialogue with global human rights visionaries. *Instinct for Freedom* (2002) traced his unlikely path from drug addiction to Buddhist monkhood in Rangoon, and then into the life of political witness.

Clements also served as the principle advisor, script consultant and co-writer for John Boorman's acclaimed film *Beyond Rangoon* (1995), which brought Burma's pro-democracy uprising to international cinema audiences.

In the years since, he has continued to expand the literary record of the struggle. *Burma's Voices of Freedom* (2019), a four-volume series co-authored with Fergus Harlow, gathered more than two thousand pages of oral histories from dissidents and former prisoners. His most recent work, *Unsilenced* (2025), resurrects Aung San Suu Kyi's moral vision from the confines of prison, placing her voice back into the global conversation on authoritarianism.

But Clements's art has never been confined to the page. He has staged spoken-word performances across North America and beyond— part theatre, part *dharma* talk, part political manifesto—weaving satire, scripture, and testimony into what he calls "psychedelic activism." On stage as on the page, he speaks with the urgency of one who believes words can save lives.

As a monk, he trained under Mahasi Sayadaw and Sayadaw U Pandita, two of the twentieth century's foremost meditation masters, and has never abandoned the *Dhamma* as his compass for political engagement. As a writer, he has spent four decades resisting erasure and amplifying what Aung San Suu Kyi once called the "Revolution of the Spirit."

Silence as a Weapon

The timing of *Conversation with a Dictator* could not be more urgent. Aung San Suu Kyi, now eighty, remains disappeared from public life. Since the February 2021 coup, she has been held in solitary confinement, dragged through sham courts, and cut off from her family. She suffers from heart disease; her son Kim Aris has reported that she may be gravely ill. For years, no one outside the junta has seen or heard her voice.

"Her silence is no accident," Clements told me. "It is the regime's engineered crime—and its most damning confession. They seek not only to erase her voice but to incinerate the memory of her existence. That is the psychology of tyranny: to kill twice—once in the body, and again in the imagination of the people."

Dictators, he explained, weaponize absence. Silence becomes their sword. Erase the voice, and you erase the memory; erase the memory, and you fracture the movement itself. This is why Clements has built his life in defiance of erasure—resurrecting the voices the regime has tried to crush.

The Making of a Witness

Clements's path to Burma was as improbable as the book he has written. Born in the United States, he fell into addiction as a young man—morphine, cocaine, nicotine, the full pharmacopeia of escape. He stumbled, half-broken, into Rangoon's Mahasi monastery in the late 1970s, where he ordained as one of the first Western Buddhist monks under Mahasi Sayadaw and later Sayadaw U Pandita. "Detox became a life," he said—a vow to stay present instead of vanish.

"I didn't come to Burma to save anyone," Clements reflected. "I came broken. The monks taught me that awareness is the highest form of courage—to stay in the fire and not turn away."

Immersed in years of relentless mindfulness training, he learned what his teachers called "moral courage as awareness." The monastery was not an escape but a crucible—where meditation was forged into a weapon of conscience.

But Burma was no sanctuary. The "rule of law" was terror. Many of his friends were imprisoned, tortured, or killed. He saw firsthand the machinery of dictatorship—and the resilience of those who resisted it.

After leaving the robes, he became first a *dharma* teacher then a journalist. His first works—*Burma: The Next Killing Fields? Burma's Revolution of the Spirit*, and *The Voice of Hope*—introduced the world to a country the generals were determined to erase.

"She wasn't simply a politician," Clements told me of Aung San Suu Kyi. "She embodied what her people call the *Revolution of the Spirit:* the fusion of conscience, courage, and compassion as a political force. She insisted we must not vilify the enemy. We must recognize the possibility of transformation in all beings—even dictators."

Aung San Suu Kyi's Feminine Revolution

It is impossible to separate Clements's new book from his decades-long dialogue with Aung San Suu Kyi. She was not only a nonviolent revolutionary in the lineage of Gandhi, King, and Mandela. She brought something else—what Clements calls the *"divine feminine"* of leadership.

"She faced her torturers without hatred," he said. "She insisted on reconciliation, on sacred reciprocity. Her mantra was simple: hope in action, love in action, compassion in action."

Her meditation teacher, Sayadaw U Pandita—who also trained Clements—became a hidden strategist of conscience, quietly guiding her and other leaders in the *Dhamma of nonviolence*. In Clements's words, he was one of the unseen architects of Burma's nationwide struggle for freedom—*a revolution infused with the intelligence of the Dhamma*.

That spirit infuses *Conversation with a Dictator*. It is a book that dares to imagine that even the most brutal tyrant may still contain the seed of transformation. "If *Ashoka* could change, why not Min Aung Hlaing?" Clements asked me, his voice carrying both challenge and hope.

Literature as Weapon

Clements calls the book a form of "psychedelic activism." Not because it is about drugs—though he is candid about the role psychedelics have played in his own healing—but because it seeks to jolt the reader out of numbness, to shatter the trance of normalized atrocity.

"This isn't punk rock," he told me. "It's existential rock—art designed to wake people up. If we can't out-create the death machine with words, images, and conscience, what chance do we have? Silence isn't neutral; it's complicity."

The book is being sent directly to world leaders and cultural figures. With his colleague Fergus Harlow, Clements has launched *UseYourFreedom.org*—a campaign to gift hundreds of copies worldwide. Among the first recipients were U.S. President Donald Trump, Julian Assange, Yoko Ono, His Holiness the Dalai Lama, Pope Leo XIV, and U.N. Secretary-General António Guterres.

"All it takes is one," Clements said. "One leader, one voice, one act of conscience. That's how revolutions turn."

The Stakes in Myanmar

Artists and musicians have been targeted. Clements's friend Zeyar Thaw—co-founder of Burma's hip hop movement and later a member of parliament—was executed last year. His crimes were poetry, music, truth itself.

"Imagine if, in America, every member of Congress and the Senate were arrested in a single night after an election," Clements said. "That's what happened in Myanmar on February 1, 2021. And instead of outrage, the world shrugged."

But Myanmar is not isolated. It is one node in a web of crises that stretch across the globe. In Ukraine, Russia's assault has torn through lives and landscapes. In Gaza, millions face the slow violence of blockade, bombardment, and genocide. In Burma as in Gaza, as in Ukraine, ordinary people are trapped between the ambitions of the powerful and the silence of the world.

"Authoritarianism always speaks in a monologue," Clements told me. "It insists on one voice, one truth, one order. But democracy—real democracy—is dialogue. It is the willingness to listen, even to those we fear or despise. Daw Aung San Suu Kyi embodied that for decades. She refused to reduce generals to demons. She insisted that transformation was possible through conversation, conscience, and compassion. She showed us that reconciliation, not vilification, is the heart of freedom."

Beyond Burma: Authoritarianism Everywhere

For Clements, Myanmar is not an isolated case. It is a microcosm of a global authoritarian turn.

"Look at Gaza. Look at Ukraine. Look at the rise of autocracy in Western nations," he said. "It's the same logic in different clothes: demonize the other, normalize atrocity, weaponize silence. Authoritarianism is government turned against its people—power inverted, consuming rather than serving."

"The lesson of Burma is not foreign," Clements continued. "It is here—in Australia, in the EU, in America. The same forces—fear, propaganda, silence—can hollow out democracies from within. The question is always the same: will we collapse into the monologue of dictatorship, or defend the dialogue of freedom? Dialogue is messy, imperfect, vulnerable—but it is the only thing that makes us human."

This is why, for Clements, the stakes of his book extend far beyond Myanmar. "We are living in an era where atrocity is being normalized," he told me. "Mass graves, bombed villages, children starved as a tactic of war—it scrolls by on our phones, and we call it news. But it is not normal. It is horror. The danger is when horror begins to feel ordinary. My work—this book—is a refusal to normalize atrocity. It is a counterspell, a reminder that nonviolence is not passive. It is the most radical weapon we have against cruelty."

He paused. "So, the question is: what does nonviolence look like in the age of atrocity? That's what I want this book to show. It's not about turning away. It's about stepping into the fire with conscience, with love, with art, with dialogue—when every instinct tells you to hate or despair. Nonviolence is resistance with a human face. And it may be the only antidote we have left."

"That's the gamble," Clements concluded. "That somewhere in Min Aung Hlaing, as in *Ashoka,* there's a fracture in the armor—a moment where grief can break through cruelty. I wrote this book for that sliver of possibility."

Toward a Film, Toward a Movement

Clements is already adapting the book into a 75-minute performance film—part spoken word, part documentary, part visual explosion. "Imagine *A Clockwork Orange* colliding with *Schindler's List* and Spalding Gray's *Swimming to Cambodia*—with perhaps a dash of *My Dinner with Andre*," he said, grinning. "And maybe even a sprinkle of AI to add a strange organic class," he added with satirical bite. Subtitled in Burmese, it is intended not only for the world but for the dictator himself.

"Transformation sounds improbable until it happens," he said. "But history shows us: it happens."

The larger vision is what Clements calls a "Virtual Live Aid for Burma"—flooding the world with conscience, harnessing artists, musicians, monks, and activists to pressure the junta. "If they can weaponize silence, then we must weaponize beauty," he told me. "That is the counter-spell."

The Revolution of the Spirit

What makes Clements unique is not only his knowledge of Burma but the moral voltage he brings to it. He speaks in a lexicon that fuses *Dhamma* and poetry, conscience and compassion, psychedelic vision and political realism.

At the end of our conversation, he returned to the phrase that has defined his work for decades: *the Revolution of the Spirit.*

"It's what Aung San Suu Kyi taught us," he said. "Revolutions aren't only political. They are existential. They are about conscience, love, redemption. That is what makes them unstoppable. Revolutions don't unfold in abstractions. They happen in letters mailed, in books smuggled across borders, in voices that refuse silence. That is how Burma will rise again."

A Call to the Reader

What does he want readers—in Santa Cruz, in New York, in London— to do?

"Read the book. Share it. Send it to someone in power. Buy ten, buy a hundred. Flood the system with conscience. *Use your freedom to amplify ours.* That is what Daw Aung San Suu Kyi asked of us. That is what this revolution requires."

The question, as always, is not whether tyranny will end. It will. The question is how much suffering it will inflict before it collapses.

Alan Clements has staked his life on reducing that suffering—one book, one conversation, one act of conscience at a time.

About the Author

John Malkin is a musician, activist, filmmaker, photographer, and radio/ print journalist based in Santa Cruz, California. For more than two decades he has hosted *Transformation Highway* on KZSC / Free Radio Santa Cruz, an independent program dedicated to exploring politics, culture, music, spirituality, and movements for liberation.

Malkin's journalism focuses on the intersections of social justice, personal liberation, and creative expression. He has written extensively about nonviolence, prison reform, war resistance, and the role of the arts in political and cultural transformation. His essays and interviews have appeared in *The Sun, Alternet, Z Magazine,* and *The Santa Cruz Sentinel,* among others.

In addition to his political and spiritual reporting, Malkin has made significant contributions to documenting music as a vehicle of resistance. He has interviewed hundreds of artists, writers, and activists associated with the punk movement, exploring the myriad ways punk has shaped activism and been shaped by it in return. These conversations were collected in his book *Punk Revolution! - An Oral History of Punk Rock Politics and Activism* (2023). The second book in his punk rock series is being released in November 2025 by Bloomsbury and is titled *Punk Spirit! - An Oral History of Punk Rock, Spirituality, and Liberation.*

As a musician and filmmaker, himself, Malkin brings a unique sensitivity to his work, bridging the worlds of art and activism. His previous books include *Sounds of Freedom: Musicians on Spirituality and Social Change* (2003) and *The Only Alternative: Christian Nonviolent Peacemakers in America* (2004).

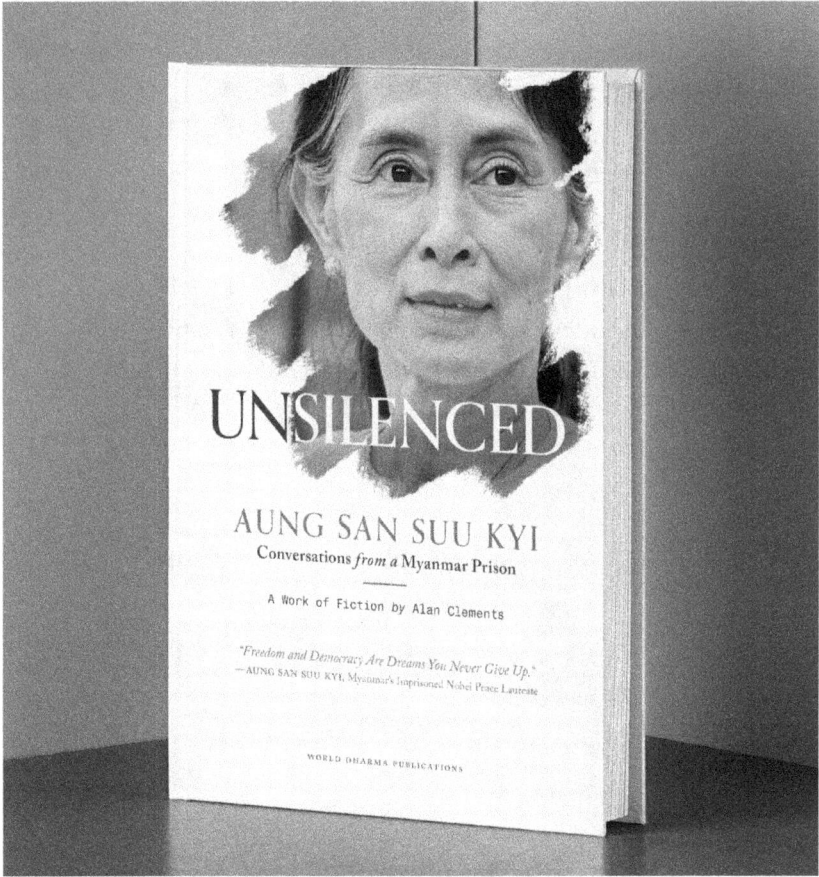

ADDENDUM II

UNSILENCED: AUNG SAN SUU KYI —
Conversations from a Myanmar Prison

A Work of Fiction by Alan Clements
World Dharma Publications, 2025

Opening Invocation: Why This Book Exists

I wrote *Unsilenced* not as literature alone, but as testimony—a vow against erasure, a refusal to collude with the silence dictatorships impose. For years, the world has heard nothing from Daw Aung San Suu Kyi: no letters, no visitors, no photographs, no proof of life. Silence has become the regime's most sophisticated weapon—a strategy of annihilation disguised as absence.

But silence, when dared, becomes freedom. Silence can be the stillness that remembers. Silence can be the aperture through which conscience speaks. Silence, inhabited with imagination, becomes resurrection—the return of voices tyrants tried to erase.

Literature is the art of defiance against disappearance. That is the wager of this book: that imagination itself can keep a leader—and a people—alive when the state seeks to annihilate not only their bodies, but their memory.

Why have I spent years of my life creating this work? Because *Burma is my Dhamma and revolutionary home.* My teachers and mentors gave me their greatest gifts—freely, unconditionally. This book is my offering back to those sacred lineages and to the unfinished future of freedom itself.

I have listened to Aung San Suu Kyi for decades, written with her, and been shaped by the same masters. The cadences of her voice live in my marrow. What you read here is fiction, yes—but fiction in service of truth, a creative act of remembrance. A testament, a requiem, and a resistance. A gift to the people of Myanmar, so their struggle is not erased. A gift to the world, so conscience is not forgotten. A gift to future generations, so they may inherit not only memory but the courage to imagine anew.

And so, *Unsilenced* is not "about" Aung San Suu Kyi. It is about the revolution of the spirit she embodied—a revolution that belongs to all of us. For authoritarianism is not confined to Myanmar. It metastasizes everywhere: in Moscow, in Tehran, in Beijing's firewalls, and in Silicon Valley's algorithms. The pathology is global; so too must be conscience.

This book is a device—scalpel, mirror, prayer. It was written to pierce the narcotic of normalization, to rupture complicity, to remind us that freedom is not bestowed from above but claimed from within.

If *Unsilenced* has a thesis, it is this: to betray conscience is the deepest corruption. When we silence conscience, we collaborate with tyranny in the most intimate way possible—we allow it to take root in ourselves. That is how dictators survive: not only with chains and guns, but with the hatred and apathy we consent to carry for them.

And so, dear reader, let me be plain: this is not a comfortable book. It is long, demanding, inconvenient. But freedom itself is inconvenient. Comfort has never saved a people; only conscience has.

A Review of *Unsilenced*: Silence and Its Discontents

Silence is never neutral. It can be imposed—as when Myanmar's generals locked their elected leader, Aung San Suu Kyi, in a cell. It can be strategic, a survival tactic of the oppressed. It can be complicit—the studied silence of democracies that look away from atrocity.

Alan Clements, in *Unsilenced*, proposes another kind: silence as resistance. His book imagines dialogues with Aung San Suu Kyi during her enforced disappearance—a feat of literary defiance meant to shatter erasure. Dictators vanish bodies; literature resurrects voices.

The architecture is hybrid: dialogues, manifestos, letters, meditations—Plato rewritten in prison garb, a Buddhist *sutta* stitched to political indictment. At its heart: conscience versus power.

The risk is clear. Is it ventriloquism to speak in Aung San Suu Kyi's voice? Clements insists not. He grounds his fiction in decades of recorded exchanges, in her speeches, in the texture of their shared teachers. The result is uncanny: her spare clarity braided with his lyric ferocity. The voice is double—imagined, yet unmistakably hers.

The central theme is what Aung San Suu Kyi once called "the revolution of the spirit." Freedom is the refusal of hatred, the endurance of dignity. Dictatorship, conversely, is predation—on imagination as much as on flesh.

Clements places her within a lineage of literary resistance: Orwell's 1984, Havel's Power of the Powerless, Baldwin's essays on the moral art of freedom. His style oscillates—liturgical one moment, prosecutorial the next. At times scripture, at times indictment.

The book's most incendiary claim is its defense of Aung San Suu

Kyi against the Western caricature of her silence on the Rohingya crisis. Clements reframes this as a moral witch hunt: scapegoating a woman who never controlled the military that committed atrocities, demanding miracles she could not perform, then punishing her when she refused to play saint for empire. Whether one agrees or not, it forces a reckoning with the ease of moral simplification.

If the book is heavy, it is because the stakes are heavy. At close to 700 pages, it demands stamina. But that, Clements insists, is the discipline of freedom. Literature that soothes cannot resist tyranny. Literature that unsettles becomes moral training. *Unsilenced* was born to break the spell of detachment and restore the intimacy of conscience.

Its final cadence is clear: Freedom is not bestowed. *Freedom must be practiced—and practiced daily—in thought, speech, and deed.*

From *Unsilenced*
Dignity, Human Rights, and the Dhamma

Author's Prelude

In her family home in Yangon, under surveillance and threat, I once sat across from Aung San Suu Kyi. Her presence was paradox—defiance tempered by grace. Her words circled back always to one truth: dignity is not given by rulers; it is claimed by conscience.

What follows is not an ordinary dialogue on politics. It is the weaving of two languages—the Universal Declaration of Human Rights and the Buddha's *Dhamma*—into a single fabric of freedom.

Alan Clements: Daw Suu, across the world we see democracy fray—from Myanmar's prisons to America's polarization, from Gaza's rubble to Ukraine's mass graves. You have often said conscience is the bedrock of leadership. How, in such a fractured age, can conscience survive?

Aung San Suu Kyi: Alan, leadership is not ambition; it is service. And service requires conscience—the quiet guide that says: Do what is right, even when fear counsels otherwise. But conscience alone is not enough. It must be trained. That is where mindfulness enters:

the discipline of attention, the refusal to look away. A leader without mindfulness is captive to fear. A people without conscience is captive to tyranny.

Alan Clements: The UDHR says dignity is the foundation of freedom. Do you see its principles as echoing the *Dhamma*?

Aung San Suu Kyi: Completely. The Declaration was written in the ashes of war. The *Dhamma* was spoken beneath a tree. But both say the same: dignity is inherent, freedom a birthright. Denied, barbarity follows. When honored, humanity flourishes.

Mindfulness turns paper rights into lived reality. It trains us to feel the suffering we'd rather avoid, to respond with integrity, to embody freedom rather than demand it from others. The *Dhamma* is not perfection—it is the practice of returning, again and again, to compassion.

Alan Clements: And what would you say to today's leaders?

Aung San Suu Kyi: I would speak softly: power is not a prize but a trust. Strength without compassion becomes cruelty; strength with humility heals. True leadership is not control but service. It is not measured by what one takes, but by what one gives.

So, I ask: Will you choose fear, or will you choose care? Will you govern for position, or will you govern for people? The answer defines not only your legacy, but our shared future.

Closing Note

To read *Unsilenced* is to enter an imagined prison cell where dictatorship cannot erase conscience. It is literature as defiance, dialogue as witness, imagination as survival. And in that cell, one hears not only Aung San Suu Kyi's voice, but the echo of our own—a reminder that freedom, if it is to survive, must be spoken, lived, and defended—again and again.

> *"Within a system which denies the existence of basic human rights,*
> *fear tends to be the order of the day... Yet even under the most crushing state*
> *machinery, courage rises up again and again, for fear is not the natural*
> *state of civilized man."*

AUNG SAN SUU KYI

ACKNOWLEDGMENTS

To Dr. Jeannine Davies, my beloved friend—whose insight, heart-intelligence, and fierce clarity have shaped the very architecture of this book. Our conversations have been lanterns on the path, illuminating places in me I had not yet dared to see. Your presence has enriched this work in ways both profound and immeasurable.

To Fergus Harlow—steadfast friend, colleague, and co-author. Your constancy, your moral voltage, and your devotion to truth and Burma's freedom movement have carried this work across thresholds I could not have crossed alone.

To Justine Elliott of Design Lasso, New Zealand—an artist of rare discernment. Your generosity, patience, and creative brilliance have lifted these pages into a realm of elegance and coherence I could only envision. It has been a privilege to walk this project forward with you.

My deepest respects to my Dhamma teachers—the late Venerable Mahasi Sayadaw and Venerable Sayadaw U Pandita — whose uncompromising rigor, boundless compassion, and relentless commitment to truth forged the inner ground from which all my work arises. Their teachings pulse through every line of my life: the revolution of awareness, the sanctity of conscience, the courage to see clearly and act wisely.

To my revolutionary family in Burma—many of whom remain imprisoned as these words are written—my heart is with you. To my long-standing friends Aung San Suu Kyi and U Win Htein, and to all unlawfully elected leaders detained in darkness: your courage continues to shape the moral horizon of the world. May this book, in whatever modest way it can, contribute to the long walk toward your freedom.

To Krystal Dyan—dear friend, colleague, and co-creator of Conversations with Visionary Women™, our inquiry into authoritarian patriarchy and the rising force of the Divine Feminine in contemporary society. Your tireless support and clarity of purpose have been a blessing and a fierce reminder of what collaborative creativity can be.

To Tom and Michelle Sewell, my long-time beloved friends—thank you for graciously and generously opening your sacred Art Studio on Maui for me to deliver the original spoken-word presentation upon which this book is based. Your kindness, your trust, and your creative sanctuary made possible the very first breath of this work.

To my beloved daughter, Bella—thank you for your quiet radiance, your patience, and your grace as you continue to explore the adventure of life. You anchor me in ways you may never fully know.

To those I have hurt or offended along the way, knowingly or unknowingly—I offer a sincere bow of apology. May we each learn, again and again, the ancient art of forgiveness and the liberating practice of reconciliation.

To my supporters and beloved friends around the world—you know who you are. This book, perhaps the most consequential of my life's work, exists because of your generosity, your trust, and your willingness to walk with me through fire and luminosity both.

In the urgency of bringing this work into being, I occasionally turned to AI for research, graphics, and editorial assistance—an imperfect tool, useful only insofar as it serves human conscience, creativity, and lived experience. Nothing replaces the beating heart of real connection.

With gratitude beyond words,
from my heart,
Alan Clements

ABOUT THE AUTHOR

Alan Clements is an author, investigative journalist, spoken-word artist, and founder of *World Dharma*. Among the first Westerners to ordain as a Buddhist monk in Burma (Myanmar), he spent nearly four years in a Rangoon monastery training in Buddhist psychology, insight meditation, and the philosophy of freedom. In 1984, Burma's dictatorship expelled him, with no reason given. He later returned as a journalist to document the regime's atrocities and the resilience of the Burmese people, until the military permanently banned his entry.

Clements co-founded The Burma Project USA/International, a pioneering human-rights and media-advocacy initiative, and the *World Dharma* Online Institute, a global program exploring "the art and activism of freedom." Inspired by Aung San Suu Kyi, its curriculum is rooted in spiritual revolution and the principles expressed in Clements's book *A Future to Believe In*.

Selected works include *Burma: The Next Killing Fields?* (1991, foreword by the Dalai Lama); co-authored with Leslie Kean, the photographic chronicle *Burma's Revolution of the Spirit* (1994, Aperture, with essays by eight Nobel Peace Laureates); and *The Voice of Hope* (1996, conversations with Aung San Suu Kyi). Other titles include *Instinct for Freedom* (2003), *Wisdom for the World* (2017), and *Burma's Voices of Freedom* (2018–2022, four volumes, co-authored with Fergus Harlow as well as) *Aung San Suu Kyi from Prison – and A Letter to a Dictator.* His later works—*Tonight I Met a Deva* (2020) and *Facing Death* (2022)—extend his lifelong meditation on conscience, impermanence, and the moral imagination. He also served as the principal advisor and script revisionist to John Boorman's acclaimed film *Beyond Rangoon* (1995).

His 2025 releases—*Conversation with a Dictator: A Challenge to the Authoritarian Assault* and *Unsilenced: Aung San Suu Kyi—Conversations from a Myanmar Prison*—spearhead the *Use Your Freedom Global Campaign*, an initiative co-created with Fergus Harlow to free Aung San Suu Kyi and Burma's more than 22,000 political prisoners. His newest work, *Politics of the Heart: Nonviolence in the Time of Atrocity—Psychedelic Activism to End War* (2025), expands his spoken-word performances into a literary act of conscience, imagination, and sacred rebellion.

As a solo satirist and performer, Clements created and toured *Spiritually Incorrect: How to Save the World, God, Drugs, Enlightenment*, raising awareness for prisoners of conscience and the "revolution of the spirit." His journalism and arts work have been featured by NBC Nightline, CBC, ABC Australia, CBS Evening News, Global National, The New York Times, The Guardian, Newsweek, Time, Democracy Now! Radio Free Asia, Yoga Journal, and others.

He has spoken at major institutions including Mikhail Gorbachev's State of the World Forum, the Soros Foundation, the United Nations Association of San Francisco, and Amnesty International's 30th Anniversary celebration at the Ford Theater in Los Angeles.

Clements received the Visioneers International Network's "Hero of Humanity" Award for lifelong service to human rights and dignity.

For more information, visit **www.AlanClements.com**
For the campaign, visit **www.UseYourFreedom.org**

Our Instinct for Freedom

"If you assume that there's no hope, you guarantee that there will be no hope. If you assume that there is an instinct for freedom, that there are opportunities to change things, there's a chance you may contribute to making a better world. That's your choice."

NOAM CHOMSKY

POLITICS OF THE HEART

Nonviolence in an Age of Atrocity—Psychedelic Activism and the End of War

What happens when theatre collides with revolution—when poetry ignites politics, when conscience refuses silence?

Politics of the Heart is a manifesto disguised as a performance—part memoir, part spoken-word theatre, part psychedelic sermon on love and defiance in an age of annihilation. It asks: *What does it mean to stay awake and human when the world itself seems addicted to destruction?*

In late 2025, in a small studio in Ha'ikū, Maui, author and spoken-word artist Alan Clements performed what he called *"a literary feature film of conscience and resistance."*

This book is the script, the meditation, and the moral aftermath of that night—a call to transform politics into a living practice of empathy and awakening.

Appearing beside two companion volumes, it completes a trilogy of conscience and revolution:

- *Conversation with a Dictator: A Challenge to the Authoritarian Assault*— an imagined dialogue with Burma's ruling general, dissecting the psychology of tyranny.
- *Unsilenced: Conversations with Aung San Suu Kyi from a Myanmar Prison*—a philosophical and spiritual meditation resurrecting the voice of Burma's imprisoned democracy leader.

Together, these works form a single architecture of defiance—a literature of resistance born from decades of witnessing dictatorship, war, and the struggle for freedom.

A former Buddhist monk, war journalist, and lifelong ally of Burma's democracy movement, Clements turns his decades of activism and spiritual practice into a blazing invocation:

Use your freedom. Use it to speak. Use it to act. Use it to love when hatred is demanded. Use it to stop the killing.

Politics of the Heart is not neutral. It is an act of conscience—a flare against the darkness, a prayer of defiance, a revolution of the spirit calling humanity to awaken before it's too late.

Alan Clements is an author, performer, and former Buddhist monk whose work merges spiritual insight with political activism. He is the author of *The Voice of Hope* (with Nobel Peace Laureate Aung San Suu Kyi), *Burma: The Next Killing Fields?* (with a foreword by His Holiness the Dalai Lama), *Instinct for Freedom*, *Unsilenced*, and *Conversation with a Dictator*. His life's work is devoted to the integration of freedom, mindfulness, and moral courage in an age of global crisis.

www.AlanClements.com | www.WorldDharma.com